Faspa

A Snack of Mennonite Stories

Eleanor Hildebrand Chornoboy

Interior Publishing & Communication Ltd.

Interior Publishing & Communication Ltd.
Box 23, RPO South St. Vital
1631 St. Mary's Road
Winnipeg MB R2N 1Z0

Printed in Canada by Tartan Graphics Ltd.
Phone (204) 736-4800 • Fax (204) 736-4700 • www.tgltd.ca

Bound in Canada by Schneider's Bindery

First printing October 2003
Second printing December 2003

Canadian Cataloguing in Publication

Chornoboy, Eleanor Gail, 1948–
     Faspa: A Snack of Mennonite Stories / Eleanor Hildebrand Chornoboy

Includes bibliographical references and index.
ISBN   0-9733958-1-8

1. Sawatzky family.   2. Hildebrand family.   3. Mennonites—Manitoba—Genealogy.
4. Manitoba—Genealogy.   I. Title.

CS89.C46 2003   929'.2'0971   C2003-905550-7

About the Title

Faspa: coffee-break, teatime; a coffee and snack time between lunch and supper.

Traditionally, Mennonite homes served *Faspa* on a regular basis. During the summer time *Faspa* was often brought to the fields where the men were working. Homemade bread, accompanied by butter, jams, and sometimes meat and cheese formed the centerpiece of *Faspa.* Frequently cakes and cookies followed the bread course. No *Faspa* was complete without coffee served with cream. When coffee was not available, *Prips* (a coffee substitute made of roasted grain) was offered. Nowadays *Faspa* is typically reserved for company on Sunday afternoons.

Faspa is not necessarily served because people are hungry or thirsty, but rather as a show of hospitality. *Faspa* offers a forum for congenial visiting, laughter, and camaraderie between family, friends, and neighbours. It is my hope that the stories in this book will create a *Faspa* of tasty little snacks that stimulate old memories and provide opportunities to tell stories of days gone by to people young and old.

Dedicated To

Adam Michele Michael Niomie Matthew Anthony Cynthia Arielle Jovain Tipelo Candace Jamie

Dear Reader,

Many things have changed since I enjoyed swinging on the swing that my Grandpa made for my little sister and me. He tied the swing from the tall cottonwoods that shaded our rural Manitoba home. More things have changed since my father grew up on the same farm with his brothers and sisters, while his father squeezed a living out of a quarter section of black soil.

Even more has changed in the time since my grandfather grew up in a nearby village. His parents had moved to Canada from the Mariopul region near the Sea of Azov in Russia (Ukraine).

So many stories about those changing times have been told and forgotten. So many stories have been told and not listened to. I regret not asking more questions and not listening more carefully to the many stories that I was told as I was growing up. This book describes what I heard when I asked the questions and listened to the answers.

My generation has focused on moving forward with little regard for what came before us. Our parents tried to tell us the stories, but we did not always hear. Now we want to know the stories and the generations after us want to know the stories. They want to be able to tell their children their family stories.

My grandparents, parents, aunts, uncles, and cousins told me some of their stories. Their experiences and way of life, described between the covers of this book, bear a resemblance to the way of life of farm families throughout the prairie provinces. There were hard times; there were good times; and there were the day-by-day rhythms.

Some stories are not a mirror image of what happened and some stories are several yarns woven together. Other stories have been remembered differently by the individual storytellers. I trust that I have captured the essence of the time and the stories. Perhaps the stories will capture your imagination.

The stories presented here are a gift for the older generation to remember, the younger generation to understand, and the new generation to learn. I sincerely hope that the stories will be read with a fondness for the past, the present, and the future.

Eleanor

Eleanor Hildebrand Chornoboy

Forward

The little vignettes in this book tell of the experiences of children and grandchildren of the early Mennonite settlers in Manitoba. Specifically, they are stories of the Peter S. and Katharina Hildebrand (born 1887 and 1889 respectively) family and the Johan M. and Helena Sawatzky (born 1891 and 1893 respectively) family.

Katharina and Peter S. Hildebrand and Helena and Johan M. Sawatzky were all children of Mennonite immigrants who had left the rich southern Russian (Ukraine) breadbasket in 1874 and 1875 to start a new life in Canada.

The pages in this book tell about moments of that first generation's children and grandchildren. Because there are different families and many people who shared similar names, some stories are prefaced with a genogram to indicate whom the story is about. The bolded names indicate who is featured in each story. In some instances, spelling of names vary according to formal documents listing the people who arrived in Canada. For more details, see "Where They Came From" (pages 205–210).

Genogram of the Hildebrand family:

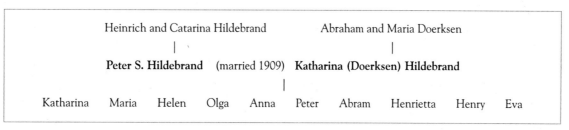

Heinrich and Catarina Hildebrand　　Abraham and Maria Doerksen

Peter S. Hildebrand　(married 1909)　**Katharina (Doerksen) Hildebrand**

Katharina　Maria　Helen　Olga　Anna　Peter　Abram　Henrietta　Henry　Eva

Genogram of the Sawatzky family:

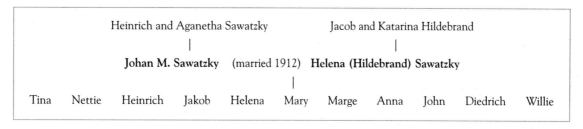

Heinrich and Aganetha Sawatzky　　Jacob and Katarina Hildebrand

Johan M. Sawatzky　(married 1912)　**Helena (Hildebrand) Sawatzky**

Tina　Nettie　Heinrich　Jakob　Helena　Mary　Marge　Anna　John　Diedrich　Willie

Table of Contents

"Churning Butter" by Mary Elias © 1997 by Pembina Threshermans Museum

Life and Times

The Mennonites brought their way of life with them to southern Manitoba when they left their farms and villages in Russia (Ukraine). The family remained the centerpiece of each custom and tradition. It was a culture of church, family, friends, hard work, and some play.

When the Peter Hildebrands and the Johan Sawatzkys were raising their children, there were no televisions or computers to amuse and entertain families. Families visited, played music, and spent leisure time visiting their friends, family, and neighbours. Local hockey teams, baseball teams, and drama productions abounded. People worked very hard, but there was always time for pleasure. On weekends, young people rushed to get their work done by late afternoon so they could go out with their friends. Despite their hard work, they had energy left to dance the night away to homemade music or to challenge the neighbouring community to a baseball game in a nearby cow pasture that doubled as a baseball diamond.

Their parents spent evenings and Sunday afternoons entertaining unannounced guests, who were always welcome. If no one came to visit on a Sunday afternoon, the parents packed up their young children and went out to visit someone. If visitors were coming along their driveway towards their house just when the parents were going out, the parents would insist that they were only going to "look at the crops". The visitors coming down their driveway absolutely had to come in for *Faspa*.

Throughout the garden's growing season, the women in the small farming community showed off their gardens to their female friends, neighbours, and relatives whenever they came to visit. The women leisurely strolled along the rows of vegetables and made U-turns at the end of each row, chatting and discussing the merits and shortcomings of the garden. Actually, the visitor extolled the virtues of the garden, praising the fullness of the pea pods and the fragrance of the summer savoury. The hostess highlighted the vices of the plot. She complained that the cabbage was splitting because it had grown too quickly and the lettuce was bitter because of the dry spring.

The women showed their gardens to each other all season long. They took their visitors to see their gardens from the moment when the first faint row of radishes began to paint a pale green line against the black soil in early spring, until the very last fat, split, orange carrot was hoisted from its summer depths. The men showed no curiosity in the gardens. Even if they were interested in the women's gardens, they pretended not to be. It was not manly to be interested in gardening unless they were bragging about the size of a cucumber or the weight of a potato.

Katharina's garden was adjacent to her sister-in-law Aganetha Hildebrand's garden. The two women regularly wandered over to each other's plots to have a little chat and to give their backs a rest from bending over to pick buckets of green beans or lifting striped beetles from the potato plants.

Their children, enough in number to make up a baseball team with substitutes, ran back and forth to each other's yards to play together and to run errands for their parents. Sharing a cup of sugar, borrowing a wrench, or chasing the cows back to where they belonged were regular activities. When the children got older, they spent evenings visiting with each other. Over the years, a hardened footpath formed between the two yards. It was shaped by the patter of bare feet, rubber boots,

– Thank you to Dave Hildebrand. On July 1, 2000, at age 83, he told the author this story about his mother Aganetha and the author's grandmother, Katharina.

work boots, and shiny Sunday shoes going back and forth between the two yards. Not a single blade of grass grew more than a tiny green inch on that path before it was flattened against the black background.

One Sunday, the neighbour, Mrs. Wall, visited Aganetha. True to tradition, Aganetha invited Mrs. Wall to see her garden. Aganetha pointed out the juicy plump red tomatoes, heavy and drooping from the vine. She showed Mrs. Wall the fine silk developing on the corn and the crop of cucumbers waiting for Monday when they would be picked and pickled. Aganetha was especially happy and just a little proud to draw attention to the tall spikes of gladiolus that were beginning to show glimmers of pink and orange.

Mrs. Wall understood Aganetha's joy and pride in her garden. She felt the same way about her own garden. She complimented Aganetha on her lovely garden and then turned to her and asked, "Aganetha, do you know what I like most about your garden?" Aganetha thought this was rather a peculiar question for a grown woman to ask another woman. She liked Mrs. Wall, so she politely replied, "No, I don't know. What do you like most in my garden?" thinking Mrs. Wall would surely select the gladiolus or the tomatoes as first prize.

Mrs. Wall smiled serenely at Aganetha. "What I like most about your garden," she said, "is the footpath that goes past your garden and Katharina's garden, all the way from your doorstep to Katharina's doorstep."

Aganetha paused for a moment. "*Na jo* (well yes)," she said with a knowing smile.

Tomorrow she would tell Katharina what Mrs. Wall had said.

Jugendverein

Peter S. and Katharina Hildebrand

|

Katharina Maria Olga Helen Anna Peter Abram Henrietta Henry Eva

The youth attending the Edenburg Church had regular gatherings known as *Jugendverein* (Youth Group). The Hildebrand girls looked forward to the event. They prepared for the evening as though it was a party. They swiped their mother Katharina's talcum powder and applied it to themselves so that some of their body parts turned to a ghostly white. They smelled good—and they could be smelled long before they were seen.

On the evenings of the *Jugendverein*, the girls made sure their dresses were ironed as crisp as fall leaves and their hair was Marcel waved as perfectly as calm ocean ripples. The girls carefully used their curling irons to wave their hair. They heated the curling irons over the kerosene lamps in their bedrooms and wrapped their hair around the irons. If the irons got too hot the hair would singe and overpower the scent of their mother's talcum powder. The Marcel waves kept a perfect shape especially well when the girls used their homemade hair gel made from flax soaked in water.

Their girlfriends in the district also went to a great deal of work to look particularly attractive for *Jugendverein*. The girl with the frizzy hair wanted desperately to have smooth hair for the evening. Before she washed her hair, she applied a thin, gooey paste of one part flour and three parts water to her dry, unwashed hair. She smoothed the mixture into her hair and let it "rest" for half an hour, after which she rinsed and washed her hair, and was left with a "no more frizz" look.

Some girls rinsed their hair in a mild vinegar solution to make their hair as shiny as a horse's mane. It was common knowledge that a few of the youths needed dandruff treatments. Dandruff was easily remedied by pouring a cup of water that had been boiled with two tablespoons thyme, over damp shampooed hair.

A few of the girls were concerned about their shiny faces. They wanted their faces to have a velvety powdered appearance. Since they could not afford those pretty compacts with the mirrors and powder puffs that they coveted in the Eaton's catalogue, they carefully fluffed a bit of cornstarch on their faces. The cornstarch toned down the shine of their soap-washed faces, and absorbed any excess oil that their faces might produce.

Just before the Hildebrand girls left the house to go to church, they rubbed their cheeks with red crepe paper to create that harvest apple blush. They knew they looked good and secretly they hoped the Edenburg boys would also notice their good looks.

On their way out the door to the church, Peter interrupted his daughters, "*Mejales, go jie tum Jugendverein fe de Kjoakj ouda fe de Junges* (Girls, are you going to the youth gathering for the church service or for the boys)?"

The girls' eyes twinkled as they covered their mouths with their hands to hide their giggles, and fibbed, "*Na oba, Papi, sejcha fe de Kjoakj* (Well, father, for the church service, of course)."

Church where the young people attended
Jugendverein in Edenburg

Loneliness and Hard Work

Peter S. and Katharina Hildebrand
|
Katharina Maria Helen Olga **Anna** Peter Abram Henrietta Henry Eva

Anna was only fifteen when she got a job with a family in Roland, Manitoba. To get to Roland, Anna boarded a train in Gretna and traveled in a passenger car to the little town that was about thirty miles to the northwest of the farm where she had grown up. Anna worked very hard for her employer. She did all the domestic work in the house. She washed all the family's laundry. She washed their heavy soiled work overalls and their delicately laced tablecloths with a scrub board and hung each washed item on the outdoor wire clothesline. Anna tended the yard. She hoed the garden, picked the vegetables, and preserved them for the winter. She prepared the meals, and then she washed the dishes in the large enamel bowl after each meal. Anna milked the cows and fed all the livestock. She was accustomed to hard work. She liked it, but she was not accustomed to the loneliness of being apart from her large family. Her employers were kind to her but they were not her people. She had always worked with her mother and her sisters. She had never heard of one person doing all the laundry and ironing by herself.

Her loneliness became desperate. She wanted so much to be with friends and her lively brothers and sisters. The only people she had anything to do with were the people she worked for and their children. Anna yearned for friendship and for someone she could joke with in *Plautdietsch* (Low German). She was not used to a household where they spoke only one language—English.

To Anna, it felt like she was on the other side of the world. She could only communicate with her Mama and Papa and her brothers and sisters by writing them letters. She was allowed to mail her letters to her family after work. She walked a few miles to town to purchase a three-cent stamp and post the letter. Anna needed to think carefully about spending money on a three-cent stamp when her monthly income was a mere $7.00.

In early December of that year, Anna used her saved money from her $7.00 monthly pay cheques to purchase Christmas presents for her family. She thumbed through the fat Eaton's catalogue and carefully chose a gift for each of her brothers and sisters and for her mother and father. She filled out the order form and added up the cost of her total order, making sure that she had enough money to pay for the gifts and three-cents left over to pay for the stamp to mail her order to the T. Eaton's Co. Her instructions were for Eaton's to send the parcel to:

Peter S. Hildebrand
Box 143
Gretna, Manitoba

Her family had no extra cash. The crops had been very poor, and the family's income was barely enough to buy the basic necessities. Christmas presents were not a basic necessity. Without Anna's gifts, not one of her little brothers and sisters would have received a Christmas present.

All the children except Anna got a gift that Christmas. Anna did not mind. She wished for only one thing—that she could be home for Christmas. Her wish did not come true. Then she wished that she would get so sick that she could not work in Roland. She could not think of any other way to go home.

Her wish came true. It came true with a vengeance. Anna became critically ill. She returned home to her family, but was so sick that she was transferred to a Winnipeg hospital. The transferring process was arduous. Bedridden Anna was transported to nearby Halbstadt, and from there, Transfer Hildebrand transported her to Emerson to catch a train to Winnipeg.

Upon her arrival in Winnipeg, the doctors determined that Anna had a ruptured appendix. She stayed in hospital in the public ward for a very long time. Anna, along with many other patients, did not receive visits from their family members because they could not afford the trip into Winnipeg. Once again, Anna was lonely. Her only visitor was Transfer Hildebrand who looked in on her whenever Anna's parents asked him to. Transfer Hildebrand went into Winnipeg regularly to deliver cattle to the stockyard. It was easy for him to drop in on Anna at the municipal hospital.

The illness took a huge toll on the young Anna. She lost a great deal of weight and she lost her hair. When it grew back, it had changed colour. The now sixteen-year-old girl grew a head of white hair. All her many nephews and nieces only ever knew Anna as their very special Auntie Anne with the beautiful white hair.

The *Gank*

– According to Herman Rempel's <u>*Kjenn Jie Noch Plautdietch? A Mennonite Low German Dictionary*</u>, a "*Gank*" is a hallway, lobby, alley, or passage.

In the Mennonite villages a *Gank* attached the barn to the house. The *Gank* was a separate room connected to the barn on one side and to the house on the other side. Sometimes when villagers walked from one part of the village to another, they took the short cut and walked through each other's *Ganks*. They simply walked through a *Gank*, said a *Gun Dach* (Good Day) if the homeowner was within talking distance, and carried on as though they were walking over a covered bridge.

During the summer months the *Gank* was used as a kitchen for all the cooking that had to be done to feed the large families. That way the remainder of the house kept cool. In the winter months the *Gank* was used to store the outer clothes and overshoes that were worn in the barn while feeding and tending to the livestock. Those clothes often got quite dirty from the manure and the feed, so most housewives did not like the soiled clothes inside the proper house. Every December the unheated *Gank* turned into a huge freezer where the housewives stored all their Christmas baking so that it would freeze and keep until Christmas. The challenge was to keep the baked goods from being eaten until Christmas. The children, who loved nothing better than their mothers' Christmas cookies, often found occasion to visit the *Gank* and just happened to find a treat that they simply had to sample. The children did not mind that the treat was frozen.

Many homes stored a variety of foodstuffs in the *Gank*. That is also where they kept their cream separators to separate the cream from the milk after each milking, morning and evening. The *Gank* witnessed the ebb-and-flow of seasons, visitors and household activity. It witnessed the history of all those who passed through it.

House and barn with a *Gank*

Johan's Warmth

Heinrich and Aganetha Sawatzky
|
Johan M. Sawatzky

Johan was softer and gentler with his grandchildren than he had ever been with his own children or his own parents. He never had words like "I love you" or "I am sorry" for his children. He had not yet learned to say those words.

When Johan's own parents moved from Manitoba to Mexico, his mother felt like a fragile rope in a tug-of-war between two strong men. All her children and grandchildren were moving to Mexico with her and her husband—except for one son. Her youngest son Johan chose to stay in Manitoba with his family. Many Mennonite families moved to Mexico in reaction to public education. Mennonite educational rights that had been granted to the Mennonites in 1873 were no longer upheld. In the July 1920 ruling, the Judicial Committee of the Privy Council in London gave Manitoba Legislation full legal sanction and determined that the Mennonites were subject to the School Attendance Act. Johan and Helena chose to stay in Manitoba. Helena was not willing to uproot her family and move away from her own

Johan Sawatzky on the train with his parents as they are leaving for Mexico in 1922
(courtesy of Nettie Neufeld)

– Told to the author by her Uncle Jakob Sawatzky on October 31, 2001.

extended family. Their children could be educated in Blumenthal. Johan and Helena did not think it was a bad thing if their children were educated in English, as long as they also learned German and studied the Catechism.

Johan and his children saw his parents off at the train station in Gretna. It ripped at his mother's heart to say good-bye to a part of herself. She ached from wanting all her family together. She had never known how to show Johan how much she loved him, but when she saw her youngest son standing at the station with his own little children in tow, she wanted nothing more than to hold him close to her. It was the only thing she could think of to do to show her son how deeply she was feeling her loss. It was not something she had ever done before, but she so wanted to hug and kiss her child good-bye. Johan was not about to permit his mother to start with any kissing and hugging at this late stage in his life. Nor was he about to let his mother know his own pain. He knew that if his mother embraced him, he would lose the strength to maintain his stoic dignity. Just as his mother leaned to kiss him, Johan stuck a cigarette in his mouth and lit it. His actions were words unspoken, but words that were deafening to his mother.

Johan's heart softened with time. When his grandchildren came along, he gave them his love in his own special way. He gave them candy, teased them gently, and held them the way he wished his mother and father would have held him when he was a young child.

Ides of March

Johan M. and Helena Sawatzky

|

Tina Nettie Heinrich **Jakob Helen Mary Marge Anna** John Diedrich Willie

The Ides of March, 1941 arrived without a hint of wind. Four-to-five inches of fresh powdery snow covered the landscape. March 15, 1941, was a glorious day.

Jakob and two of his younger sisters, Mary and Helen, decided to take advantage of the lovely day to go to the nearby village of Sommerfeld to see Mr. Hildebrand, the *Trachtmoaka* (the right maker or bone fixer, also known as a chiropractor). It was not unusual to visit *Trachtmoaka* Hildebrand whenever anyone had a few aches and pains.

Jakob hitched his favourite horse Daizie to the cutter, a type of horse drawn sleigh. They would ride on the sleigh to Sommerfeld. Mary and Helen bundled up in heavy coats and warm hats. Their younger sisters, Marge and Anna, waved good-byes, wishing they could go too. Just before the three youths left their farmyard, their father took a photograph of them in the sleigh. He wanted a photograph of his children, but he was just as interested in recording the new fresh March snow.

There was an awful lot of new white powdered snow covering the landscape, considering it was already March.

Around 6 p.m., Jakob giddy-upped the horse and off went the three Sawatzky adolescents. Daizie's hooves kicked up just a little bit of the fluffy snow into the faces peeking through the woolen scarves and hats. Jakob commented to his sisters, "*Wie woare de Township Road näme* (We'll take the Township Road)." A half-mile north of their yard, Jakob would turn west on the township road that would take them directly to the north end of Sommerfeld.

The township road was the most commonly traveled road, but on that day it had no visible tracks from the day's traffic. Everything was white except for the shadowed outcroppings of farmyards with planted rows of trees. It looked as though God had taken a monstrous white down-filled quilt and gently laid it over all of Blumenthal. The road had no telephone poles or fence posts to point

Jakob with Mary and Helen (courtesy of Jakob Sawatzky)

In a letter sent to the author by her Uncle Jake Sawatzky, March 2002, he included the photograph taken on March 15, 1941.

On the back of the photo, Jakob wrote:

"1941 March 15   On our way to Sommerfeld. The night of a big snow storm. This is the place where I was born and raised. It's me Jakob J. Sawatzky and my two sisters Helen and Mary. The horse's name is Daizie."

Further:

"This is the same horse and sleigh I went to visit Mom (Helen Abrams, Jakob's first wife) for the first time.
It was 1940, 2 weeks before Christmas."

the traveler in the right direction. That March 15th, the road only had beautiful white soft snow on it, making it feel as though they were riding in Paradise.

They took their time, enjoying the muffled sound of Daizie's hooves in the snow, chatting about local events and enjoying all that nature had spread out for them. It was a perfect day, and as they neared Sommerfeld, the spring sun was approaching the horizon and saying its good-night to the three young sleigh riders.

When they arrived at the *Trachtmoaka* Hildebrand's yard in Sommerfeld, Mr. Hildebrand greeted them at the front gate. He instructed Jakob to tie the horse to the railing and come inside. Mr. Hildebrand turned around to go back into his house, leaving Jakob and his sisters to tie up the horse. They would follow the *Trachmoaka* inside as soon as Daizie was tethered.

Without even a hint of warning, the weather, that had been so kind, took a very sudden turn. The wind picked up the snow by the shovelfull and blasted it against anything in its path. By the time Mr. Hildebrand had made the few paces back into his house, he turned back to the three Sawatzky youths and shouted to them so he could be heard above the raging wind, "*Brinj jün Peat enn dee Schtohl nen. Jie woare fonn doag nijch no Hüs reise* (Take your horse into the barn. You will not be traveling home today)." The three raced to get out of the storm and into *Trachmoaka* Hildebrand's home.

The wind was ferocious. It lifted up mountains of snow and hurled it into the air, making it nearly impossible to see anything beyond the length of an arm. The three Sawatzky youths thanked God that they had not left their home in Blumenthal

any later. Even a three-minute delay would have left them out in the storm without being able to see the road or their horse in front of them. They would have been traveling blindly.

Their parents were at home, sick with worry. They had ardent conversations with God, asking him to protect their three children Jakob, Mary and Helen.

Five minutes after the youths were in the Hildebrand home, that reeked of the *Apodoldok* used for the *Trachtmoaka* therapy, Mr. Jacob Hildebrand came to the door, asking "*Senn de Hauns Sawatzjes Kjinja aul bot hia* (Have the Johan Sawatzky children arrived)?"

Johan Sawatzky had telephoned Old Karl Hildebrand, who had the only government telephone in Sommerfeld, inquiring after the safety of his children. Johan was very concerned that they may have been caught in the storm that had put Blumenthal into a total whiteout.

Old Karl Hildebrand's government telephone allowed him to receive phone calls from outside the village of Sommerfeld. He also had a party line, which allowed him to phone local villagers. Using the party line, he phoned the message to Jacob Hildebrand who in turn delivered the message to *Trachtmoaka* Hildebrand.

Messages were sent from one party line to another. When a telephone was not available, the villagers walked from home to home, delivering messages.

When Jacob Hildebrand delivered this message of concern to *Trachtmoaka* Hildebrand, he told Jakob to make sure that Old Karl Hildebrand would phone Johan Sawatzky to let him know that his children were safe and sound, but they would not be returning home to Blumenthal that night.

The three young people stayed at *Trachtmoaka* Hildebrand's home until midnight, when the storm had lost some of its might. Jakob went outdoors to hitch up Daizie. He had decided they would stay with their own grandparents and their Aunt Anne and Uncle Cornelius and their children who all lived together in Sommerfeld. Surely it would be more fun to stay with their cousins and grandparents than with *Trachtmoaka* Hildebrand and his wife. They were very nice people, but it would just be more fun at their grandma and grandpa's place.

The storm was not over, but Jakob was confident that they could safely get to their grandparent's home, which was just a few yards away from the *Trachtmoaka*. Jakob could barely see the tops of the trees, but Daizie took the lead. Daizie had been to their grandparents' yard many times before. This was very familiar territory to her. Jakob believed Daizie had a better idea of how to get to his grandparents' yard than he did.

The three youths looked forward to staying at their grandparents' house because they knew it would be warm and comfortable there. Their grandmother always had special treats. The young people knew that their grandparents would be very pleased to see them, and that they would receive that extra special attention that only grandparents can give. Their grandparents' house was always warm and smelled of homemade soups and freshly baked buns Alas, when they arrived that stormy night, they wished they had stayed away. It would have been better for them to stay at the Apoldodok smelling *Trachtmoaka* Hildebrand's home. Their grandparents' home was cold and filthy. It looked like it had been ransacked by an evil chill. The chimney had burned out from an excessive soot build-up. Black soot that had lined the chimney covered the walls, the floors, and the furniture. Even their grandmother's usually crisp apron and her gartered stockings were sooty and smudged. There was no heat in the building. All that the three young people wanted to do was to warm up and be comforted. They stayed at their grandparents' house, but it was a long and cold night.

By morning the storm had lost all its energy. As quickly as he could, Jakob hitched Daizie to the sleigh and he and his two sisters bundled up to go back home to Blumenthal, where they knew the house would be warm and clean. They hoped that their sisters might have some steamy noodle soup waiting for them.

On their way home, they were in awe of the prairie painting that God had prepared for them. The snow looked like a sea of glistening diamonds in the brilliant morning sun. There was not a single sign of the wind's wrath from the night before. All was calm.

Days after they got home, they learned that their neighbour Arthur Parent's three head of cattle were found suffocated in the middle of their farm. The cattle had died in the March 15th snowstorm. It was a harsh reminder of the fragility of life and of the power of a March snowstorm. The three young people and their parents thanked God for their good fortune. The family was safe.

Country Gardening

Peter S. and **Katharina** Hildebrand
|
Henry

Johan M. and Helena Sawatzky
|
Anna

Katharina loved her gardens—her vegetable garden to feed her family, and her flower garden to nourish her soul. Her flower garden bloomed from the fresh early spring until the crisp late autumn. Spring welcomed fragrant lavender lilacs, perky, vibrant tulips and heavy-headed fuchsia peonies. The summer delivered saucy little multi-coloured Bachelor Buttons and aromatic Sweet Williams next to the cheery purple-and-yellow pansy faces. Every day when Katharina looked out her front door, her eyes feasted on her flower garden.

Katharina thrilled to spend warm days in her vegetable garden, watching the green rows of peas, beans, carrots, and watermelon grow taller and wider by the day. Each row of vegetables was straight as an arrow, and tended by Katharina. She coaxed the seedlings to grow and produce enough food for her summer and winter tables.

The first plants that Katharina could serve her family were the lettuce leaves. She washed the freshly cut lettuce to make sure that no green worms were nestled in the crevasses of the leaves. Then she smothered the lettuce in a tangy mixture of sugar, vinegar and thick farm cream. The best flavours in the mouth were when that salad was served next to new potatoes boiled in their skins, *Schmaunt Fat* (cream gravy) and smoked *Schinkje Fleesch* (ham).

Katharina waited impatiently for her garden to offer her crisp green beans and tender little peas. She could hardly wait until the day when she and her daughters could make fresh *Jreene Schauble Sup* (Green Bean Soup) flavoured with smoked pork and new shoots of summer savoury.

Nothing tasted more delicious than that first bowl of soup from the garden's bounty. It was truly a gift from God.

Katharina's cabbages grew and grew until the heads got so large that they split. Before any of the precious cabbage went to waste, Katharina and her daughters shredded the cabbage and let it ferment in large oak barrels to make sauerkraut. The sauerkraut froze in the barrels in late fall. When Katharina made *Sauerkraut Borscht* during the winter, she hacked a frozen mass of the fermented cabbage out of the barrel and added it to her sumptuous pork broth, flavoured with dried dill from her garden.

Katharina spent the lion's share of the summer, preserving garden produce for winter. She dried beans for bean soup; she pickled watermelons in barrels; and she dried swaths of dill, parsley, and summer savoury.

When Katharina retired from the farm, she left her garden to her son Henry's wife, Anna. Ever since Anna had married Henry, she had helped Katharina with the gardening—hoeing the weeds, picking bugs off the potato plants, picking beans, and dusting the tomato plants for bugs, but Anna had never gardened all by herself.

Nonetheless, Anna thought she knew all about gardening. In early spring, armed with her youthful wisdom, she planted her garden just as her mother-in-law had done. Anna got out the long string that had sticks tied to each end. She stuck one stick into the ground at one end of the garden, unwound the string as she walked to the other end, and stuck the second stick into the ground. Anna made sure the string was taut, marking a row as straight as her school ruler. The string showed Anna where the furrow for the seed should be so that her rows of vegetables would be as straight as Katharina's had been.

The warm sun and gentle rains helped Anna's garden grow like Jack's beanstalks. Everything looked great—except for one thing. Anna had failed to notice Katharina's strategic plan of where vegetables were planted within the garden's borders. Katharina never seeded pumpkins in the middle of the garden. That, however, was exactly what Anna had done. The pumpkin vines spread over the entire garden, reaching out to all the other veggies. Anna would not tolerate any

– Story told to the author by her Mother, Anna Hildebrand on July 20, 2002.

bullying in her garden. Like a knight fighting a dragon, she chopped off the far-reaching pumpkin vines that were wrapping their throttling tendrils around all the other vegetables. The pumpkins were not daunted. Anna had limited their space, but they still produced enough pumpkins for the entire community. There were enough pumpkins from Anna's garden, for everyone in the district to have pumpkin pies, pumpkin seeds, and scary Jack-o-lanterns. The next year she planted the pumpkins far away from all the other vegetables in her garden.

Anna Hildebrand's garden 2003

Jreene Schauble Sup
(Green Bean Soup)

1 smoked meaty ham bone or farmer sausage
Twigs of summer savoury
6 cups green beans, cut fine
2 medium carrots, sliced
2 medium potatoes, diced
1 small onion, shredded
1 cup peas, shelled

Cover the ham bone or sausage with water. Add the summer savoury and cook until the meat is falling-off-the-bone tender.

Add salt and pepper to taste.

Add the vegetables and cook until all the vegetables are tender.

Remove the summer savoury before serving.

Some folks like to add a little cream to their bowl of soup.

Serve with fresh homemade buns

Christmas Presents

Johan M. and **Helena** Sawatzky
|
Tina Nettie Heinrich Jakob Helena Mary Marge Anna John Diedrich Willie

Christmas was the very best time in the whole year for Helena and Johan Sawatzky's children. What would the *Naetklos* (Santa Claus) bring them? The children knew that the *Naetklos* brought them pretty much the same thing every Christmas, but they did not mind. They were excited, and there would be something special in each child's Christmas bowl.

Every year each child found a pair of homemade slippers in their Christmas bowl. All the slippers were identical except for the size. Red paint emblazoned the shoe size on the leather sole of each slipper. That way, each child knew exactly which slippers were his or hers, and there was no need to argue about which slipper belonged to whom.

Besides the slippers, each child also found one toy in the bowl. It was the early 1930s and there was no extra cash to buy toys for each child in a large family. Helena, and every other mother in the district, had to be very creative in making her

children's Christmas joyful and memorable. The toys in the children's bowls were the same toys they had received the year before, and the year before that. During the fall when the children were busy on the farm and in school and less occupied with their toys, Helena quietly put away her children's toys where they could not find them. She let them believe that they must have lost their toys, and they would have to look very hard to find them. She did not let on that she had hidden them away so that she could refurbish them for the Christmas bowl.

Every year, just before Christmas, Helena invited her children's aunts, *Sauntji Mum* (Aunt Susan) and *Tien Mum* (Aunt Tina), to help her spruce up her daughters' dolls so that they would have another year's play in them. Helena left the boys' toys up to her Johan to look after.

Sauntji Mum repainted the doll heads attached to the soft stocking doll bodies. She used her fine brushes and enamel paints to repaint the pretty

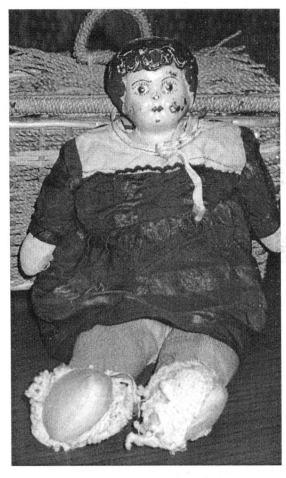

Doll with metal head and homemade clothes
(courtesy of Anna Hildebrand)

tin faces and tin hair. There was one tin doll head with a stocking doll body for each little girl in the family. The renewed dolls had hair colour changes, and their blue eyes turned to brown. *Sauntji Mum* made each doll *sea schmock* (very pretty).

While *Sauntji Mum* painted faces and hair, *Tien Mum* and Helena sewed new clothes for the dolls with the freshly painted faces and hair. The room where the women stitched and painted buzzed with activity. No children were allowed in the room, but the women were caught up in their children's contagious excitement. They could hardly wait to see the little girls' faces light up when they saw their dolls with fresh faces and beautiful new clothes. The children made up many excuses so that they could come into the room because they knew something good was going on behind the closed door. Helena reminded her youngsters, "*Nü mott jie hee büte bliewe, ooda kjemmpt de Naetklos goanig hia häa* (Now you must stay out of here, or Santa Claus won't come)."

Each doll was dressed in a new frock trimmed with lace and buttons that had been rescued from worn out clothes. The frocks were made of scraps left over from dresses and aprons that Helena and her oldest daughters had sewn for the little girls in the family. It was very special when the doll's dress looked just like her new "Mommy's" dress. Helena decked each doll out in stockings and crocheted booties. The dolls were just like new.

Christmas morning was everything the little children had hoped for. There in the bowl beside the slippers was a freshly repaired and painted tractor or truck for the boys, and a beautiful doll for each little girl. The children loved their tractors and dolls. The little girls had new babies to play with. They would take very good care of them and treat them with all the love they deserved.

Mary   Marge   Anna

Three little girls who couldn't wait to see their Christmas presents

Family Gatherings

Johan M. and **Helena** Sawatzky
|
Tina Nettie Henry Jakob Helen Mary Marge Anna John Diedrich Willie

Helena and Johan's family traditionally celebrated Christmas and Easter on the *tweede Heljedach* (second holiday), meaning they gathered on Boxing Day, and on Easter Monday. Christmas day and Easter Sunday were the lull before the storm for Helena and Johan. On the day of the *tweede Heljedach*, Helena and Johan's little two-story farmhouse with the brick veneer bulged with children and adults ranging in size from infant to double–X large. Attendance at a family gathering was not optional except for those who were giving birth or on their deathbed. The house buzzed with the children's raucous play. The teenagers skulked into an upstairs bedroom and guarded the door to keep their pesky little brothers and sisters from entering. The mothers talked over the din of their crying babies and demanding toddlers. The fathers sidled into the living room to find a comfortable chair while there was still space.

Mealtimes had the same order, gathering after gathering. The women bustled about the kitchen preparing food, setting the table, and keeping a watchful eye over their little ones. Johan and the men sat in the living room, *spatsearing* (visiting) and smoking. On occasion, one of the men popped his head into the kitchen, reminding his wife that their baby's diaper still needed changing.

When the meal was ready and the table set, Helena called Johan and the younger men to the large kitchen table. They sat down to a table laden with a big bowl of beefy *Komst Borscht* (Cabbage Soup) flavoured with dill from Helena's garden and platters of pale chicken pieces with raisins and prunes, roasted in lard. Johan sat at the head of the table and the younger men surrounded the remainder of the table. The men quickly bowed their heads in unison as though an invisible angel had given them a signal to say a silent grace. The women served their men coffee and milk, and kept the bowls of *Borscht* and the platters of chicken brimming. The men dished up their plates, passing the bowls around the table like the second hand on Johan's cuckoo clock.

The men finished eating in no time. After all, they were farmers, or at least they were all from the farm. The purpose of the noon meal was to fill the hollow stomachs. The food was not to be savoured and lingered over while they debated world affairs. That discussion could wait until they returned to the living room to smoke and *spatsea* some more. After the men left the table, the women refilled the bowls and platters and sat down to eat. Each woman sat in the same warm seat that her husband had just vacated. The women sometimes got themselves clean cutlery from the drawer with the wooden dividers, but they generally ate from the unwashed plates their husbands had left. The women did not take long to eat either, because their hungry children were impatiently waiting for their turn at the table. Occasionally an errant child tugged at his mother's elbow with a "*Mie hungat. Kjenn wie boolt äte* (I'm hungry. Can we eat soon)?" The mothers greeted those words with stern looks and sharp tongues. There was no allowance for rude behaviour. Their children had to learn patience and good manners. They should wait until the mothers were done eating. There were no exceptions.

When it was finally the children's turn to eat, they sat where their mothers had sat, and they ate from their mother's unwashed plates. However, most mothers had more than one child, so some children got the coveted clean plates and cutlery.

Very soon after everyone had finished *Meddach* (the noon meal), the women started to prepare *Faspa* (a coffee and snack between lunch and supper). *Faspa* always brought homemade buns, dill pickles, coffee, jams, butter, cheese, cookies, and cakes to the table. The children knew that everything except the butter and cheese was homemade.

A family gathering meant no holiday for the women. And yet, they had a good time. They enjoyed the gatherings. The kitchen buzzed as Helena's daughters and daughters-in-law worked and chatted. They shared family news, shyly boasted about their children's latest accomplishments, and exchanged recipes. Whenever the chance arose, they told funny stories and played jokes on each other and gossiped just a little bit. Sometimes, if the children listened carefully to their mothers in the kitchen, they could hear faint whispers followed by roars of female laughter. When the children or the men asked what was funny, the women's only response was "*Ach, Yretji fetaled ons waut* (Oh, Marge told us something)." The women simply smiled, and carried on with their chatting.

Family gatherings molded the centerpiece of what it meant to be a family. It was a time for renewing ties. It was a time for the children to learn about their family's values. It was a time to strengthen the fabric of the family and a time to teach the children how to create their own family ties.

Komst Borscht
(Cabbage Soup)

2 pounds meaty beef bone
12 cups cold water
1 medium head cabbage, chopped fine
2 medium potatoes, cubed
1 small onion, minced
Sprigs of fresh dill or dried dill
1 tsp. salt
1/2 tsp. sugar
Pepper to taste
1 bay leaf
 a few sprigs parsley
2 cups tomato juice or stewed tomatoes
1/2 cup cereal cream

Boil the beefy meat bone for at least 1 1/2 hours.

Add vegetables and seasonings. Cook until vegetables are done.

Add tomato juice or stewed tomatoes. Bring to a boil. Serve.

Cream can be added to individual bowls at the table.

The soup tastes better each time it is reheated.

Tweede Heljedach (Second Holiday)

Johan M. and Helena Sawatzky
|
Diedrich and Bernice Sawatky
|
Ricky

After Johan passed away, Helena moved into a tiny two-bedroom bungalow in Altona. The house had no basement. It was so small that the lawn swing with the two seats stretched halfway across the front of her house. There was not a chance that all her children, grandchildren and great-grandchildren could crowd into that elf-sized house for the usual Christmas celebration on Boxing Day. Goodness sakes, there were more than sixty people in number.

Tweede Heljedach (second holiday or holy day), commonly known as Boxing Day, was the day after Christmas. Helena's grandchildren called that day "Grandma Sawatzky Christmas". It was the day when she and Johan had always had their family gathering with all the children ever since she and Johan had become grandparents. She would never let that tradition fall by the wayside. She rented the auditorium of the Elmwood School in Altona. Then everyone could fit in without feeling like they were inside a sealed sardine can. They gathered in the large room that doubled as a gymnasium and an auditorium. At one end of the room, the four feet high stage was framed with shiny up and down brown planks. It was perfect because then each of Helena's grandchildren stood right in the middle of the stage when they said their Christmas *Wensch* (wish). A Christmas *Wensch* was a Christmas poem or a Christmas Carol the children had learned at school or at Sunday School. The very little ones learned their *Wensches* on their mothers' knees. Each little one performed their *Wensch* in front of their grandma and all the aunts and uncles and cousins. Only the babies who were feeding at their Mommy's breast did not have to say a *Wensch*.

After a huge Christmas dinner of pale roasted chicken with *Bobbat*, a raisin dressing served with the chicken, the dishes were washed and towel dried by all the Mommies. The children ran about in the gym with wild screaming, laughing, and shouting. It was so much fun. They did not see their cousins very often and they wanted to spend every moment playing. The auditorium was so big that they could run, play tag, build castles with the chairs, and pretend they were monsters or knights in shining armour. Meanwhile, the Dads sat in little groupings discussing current events such as the price of wheat and how the Toronto Maple

Leafs were doing in the league.

Immediately after the women finished washing and drying the dishes, they called their children to line up to say their Christmas *Wensch* in front of their grandmother. "*Nü mott jie jüne Wensche opsaje* (Now you must recite your wish)." The children did as they were told, but it was much more fun to play. They knew that their grandmother would give them each a goodie bag filled with an orange, candy and peanuts. She would also give each child a quarter, but the children just wanted to play. They were having such a good time. Nonetheless, Kirby played "*O Tannenbaum*" on the accordion; he had learned it for his Sunday School concert. Elma sang "Away in a Manger". Irene recited a poem she had memorized for the school concert, and little Valerie stood up on the stage nervously twisting her skirt with her pudgy little fingers until her frilly panties showed. Ricky knew his cousin Dale didn't like this very much either, but Dale's Mommy and Daddy made sure he said his poem too.

Some children loved to perform for all the big people. Other children wished they could turn into a mouse that no one could find until the *Wensching* was over for them. They thought that it was a horrible thing to be there in front of all those people. For Ricky, this was the blackest spot on his Christmas calendar. Even if his grandma had given him a whole dollar instead of the twenty-five cents for his performance, it would not have been enough to pay Ricky for his agony.

His older sister Lynn breezed through her rendition of "Johnny Appleseed". She loved to be on stage. She wanted to be a movie star. Ricky's turn came right after Lynn's sparkling performance. He hated this. It was so scary in front of all those old aunts and uncles and all those millions of cousins. Lots of cousins were really old and they spoke that funny *Plautdietsch* just like his grandma did. He did not know what they were talking about. He was so happy that his little cousins and he all spoke the same way—in English.

– This story is dedicated to the memory of Rick Sawatzky. It made him smile.

His Mommy spent a long time practicing with him. At home when he was playing with his Tonka tractor and riding his little tricycle in the basement, he sang his song all by himself. He did not need his Mommy to help him. His Mommy and Daddy were so proud of him when he did it all by himself. He liked it when they said those gushy things to him about what a good job he did. He sang:

Twinkle twinkle little star
How I wonder what you are
Up above the sky so high
Like a diamond in the sky
Twinkle twinkle little star
How I wonder what you are.

He even sang the song to himself when they were driving in Daddy's big car to Grandma's place that very morning. He knew that song like he knew how to button his new Christmas shirt all by himself.

He stood in the line with all the other kids to say his *Wensch*. When his turn came, he slowly walked onto the middle of the stage with his face pointing towards his toes. His face stayed pointing in that direction. There was no way he would look up at all those people no matter how much his Mommy said "Ricky, look up. Look at Grandma." Oh, how he wished he could stutter like his Daddy so that he wouldn't have to sing to Grandma and all those big people. His mouth was dry like the time he had run very fast in the hot sun. It felt like there were many bugs flying around in his tummy.

Ricky started to sing "Twinkle, Twinkle", but his voice was so soft he could hardly hear himself. His eyes were brimming to the very edge with big wet salty tears, and his voice was getting lost in his throat. Ricky stopped singing and ran off the stage into his Mommy's arms. He knew he would never be an actor or a singer. He would be a truck driver.

Ricky got his 25 cents and a goodie bag anyway. He went off to play with his little cousins Ernie and Dale and Timmy and Eddy and Harvey. That was a lot more fun than standing alone in front of all those people. His little cousins agreed with him.

Butchering Bees

During the long, sweltering summer, farm families in southern Manitoba raised their little suckling piglets to become big fat grown-up pigs. They fed them plenty of *Schroot* (chopped grain) mixed with water and scraps from the same garden that contained enough vegetables to feed large families. The pigs were raised for the sole purpose of being butchered in the fall to feed the families during the long winters ahead of them. The pigs were not kept in germ free hog barns that lined up in long rows with no room to walk about. The pigs were kept in small barns that had a pig-sized exit to an outside fence so that they could roam freely between the indoors and the outdoors. While the pigs were on this earth, their lives were quite comfortable. They had food served to them by the bucketful; they had their living space cleaned for them; and they could choose their location of relaxation—inside or outside. Life was good until late fall.

In late fall, the pigs made the supreme sacrifice at the hog butchering bees. Households invited their friends, family and neighbours to help butcher the pigs they had fattened. The butchering bee lasted all day, starting in the early frosty morning and finishing when the sun was approaching the western horizon. Butchering was a fall event because in fall the weather cooled enough to store the meat without it spoiling. The meat kept so that the family had pork for months ahead.

The day before the bee, the host family ensured that everything was ready for the event. The knives were honed to razor sharpness, and the garage or shed where the butchering took place was swept clean of all debris and lingering cobwebs. Large sheets of plywood were set on wooden carpenter horses to create makeshift tables. The *Miagrope* (a large cauldron set on a brick and mortar fireplace) was scrubbed to a velvet gleam. Ample wood was chopped and gathered to keep the fire in the *Miagrope* burning all day long. The scalding trough stood washed and set up outside. If everything was not ready for the day's work, people regarded the host family as slovenly, disorganized, and a

Miagrope

little lazy. No one wanted that reputation. The hosts made very sure everything was ready and in its place. Then the butchering would surely run smoothly and the family's reputation as being diligent people would be safeguarded.

The woman of the household prepared all the cooking and cleaning utensils for the bee. She spent days baking bread, cakes, and cookies to feed the helpers. She prepared enough food to serve all the helpers breakfast, dinner at noon, and *Faspa*.

On the day of the butchering bee, the host family arose very, very early. The woman started breakfast, and the man started the fire in the *Miagrope* that had been filled with water the night before. The man, and any children old enough to help, fed the farm animals and milked the cows before any guests arrived.

The guests and their sleepy children arrived before the sun showed its complete face in the east. Upon their arrival, breakfast was waiting for them. Boiled coffee with fresh cream; homemade raspberry, strawberry, rhubarb, and saskatoon jams, made from the summer's harvest and freshly baked buns. Some women even made *Dwoj* (little hand–rolled balls of homemade cottage cheese seasoned with caraway seed). No guest left the breakfast table feeling hungry.

The men ate breakfast first. They did not linger long over the meal. Their work started before the women came outside to do the women's part in the butchering. The men quickly dressed in their warm jackets, their farmer caps and water-proofed boots and went into the frosty air to start the day's work.

The pigs chosen for the year's dining pleasure were lured to the feeding trough and shot with a .22 calibre rifle. Men dragged and lifted the pigs into a water-tight wooden butchering trough that was large enough to hold one pig at a time. Boiling water from the *Miagrope* was poured over the freshly killed pig. The men scraped each bristly

hair off the entire pig, making the skin smooth and shiny like a baby's ankle. The men used sharpened discs attached to wooden handles to shave the pigs. The shaver looked like a flattened old school bell.

Once shaved, the men unceremoniously hoisted the pig by its hind trotters, and hung it up and eviscerated it. Not just anyone knew how to eviscerate a pig. When a man demonstrated skill in gutting a pig, he and his wife received invitations to an unusual number of butchering bees in the community and neighbouring communities. One young man received twenty such invitations in a single butchering season.

The carcass was halved and brought into the shed where the women waited with their razor-sharp knives. They cut all the meat from the bones. Every part of the pig had a use. Nothing was wasted. Pork hocks and tongues were pickled, parts of the head turned into head cheese, and intestines, well cleaned, would be used as sausage casings. By the end of the day, a pig running around on all four trotters was turned into bacon, ham, *Jreewe* (cracklings), farmer sausage, liver sausage, ribs, and pork roasts.

Layers of fat, cut from the large pieces of meat on the makeshift table, were tossed into the hot *Miagrope* that had been dried and wiped clean from the morning's boiled water. The fat slowly melted into clear liquid lard. It was scooped into tin cans, pails, and jars to harden. The hard white lard lasted all winter and through the following summer.

A family received a degree of status in the community by owning the fattest pig. Housewives used plenty of lard for baking the finest flaky pie crusts, for making airy loaves of bread, and for roasting meat. No housewife used cooking oil or olive oil. She used lard.

While the fat was rendered, meaty ribs were added to it. As soon as the ribs were cooked, they were lifted out of the fat, and left to cool. Children looked forward to having the *Rebspäa* (ribs) the very evening of the butchering.

Little pieces of meat remained swimming in the little bit of leftover lard at the bottom of the *Miagrope* after the clear lard was scooped into containers. These fatty *Jreewe* (cracklings) were ladled into tin cans. *Jreewe* was a popular fried breakfast menu item served with bread and sometimes with Chokecherry *Tsoppsel* (thin wild cherry syrup).

One woman tended the rendering lard by stirring it with a long metal rod with a flat metal semi-circle welded to the stirring end. Other women cleaned the intestines with salt and bran for encasing the sausage meat. Everyone had a task. The meat from the pig's jowl was minced with salt, pepper and liver, and placed into the sausage maker. The sausage maker pushed the meat into a cleaned large intestine, creating *Läwa Worscht* (liver sausage). The *Läwa Worscht* was boiled in water and was best when eaten cold.

A stainless steel meat grinder minced the chunks of meat. The meat was seasoned with just the right amount of salt and pepper, and ladled into a sausage maker. A slippery rumpled intestine was slipped onto the sausage maker spigot like a too-long sleeve rumpled over a little child's arm. Slowly, pressure applied to the sausage maker lever, squirted the seasoned meat through the spigot into the intestine, forming nicely rounded farmer sausages. As the meat filled the intestine, the sausages got longer and stiffer, unfurling like a clown's balloon wiener dogs.

At noon the working guests ate a large meal. Common fare was roast chicken, boiled potatoes, gravy, vegetables, and pie for dessert. They ate in shifts—the men first, the women second, and children last. No one took any extra time to eat. They all wanted to finish the work before they had to go home to feed their chickens, slop their hogs, and milk their cows. They also wanted to be home

to greet their school age children who would be coming home after four o'clock.

As the day drew to a close, the men smoked the meat. They hung the farmer sausages, the hams that had not been ground into sausages, and slabs of skin with fatty marbled meat soon to become bacon, in a smoke house the size of an outhouse. A smoky oak fire flavoured and preserved the sausages and hams to peak perfection. The sausages only took a few hours to smoke, but the large hams covered in fat and a thick pig skin took several days to be smoked to the bone.

Before the guests left at the end of the day, they were served *Faspa*. *Faspa* was similar to breakfast with plenty of fresh coffee, buns, jams, cakes, cookies, and sometimes homemade cottage cheese. As the guests departed, the host couple gave them thank you presents of a few ribs of the *Rebspäa* or a ring of *Läwa Worscht*.

Different households had various customs when

they butchered. Johan Sawatzky and his wife Helena invited all their grown children and their grandchildren home for the day when they held their butchering bees. They planned for the bee to take place on November 11 so that the school children could join them immediately after they had had their Remembrance Day services in school. The grandchildren played in the snow, and the adults worked. Johan made sure that on that day there was plenty of *Mumpkje's Wien* (married-woman's wine) for all. *Mumpkje's Wien* was a syrupy sweet cherry non-alcoholic cider. It was such a grown-up treat for the children. The children thought it so "adult" to drink *Wien* (wine). When the adults went indoors to have their noon meal, some children helped themselves to a little extra *Mumpkje's Wien*. On occasion, they even pinched a little taste of the freshly cooked *Rebspäa* without explicit permission.

The children ate after the adults finished their noon meal. They thought the *Rebspäa* and *Mumpkje's Wien* were much tastier than their grandma's white chicken with raisins.

Butchering bees were community activities. They were a time to work and visit together, and an effective way to accomplish large tasks. The bees are remembered with a fondness for community and for the way things were done.

Drawing of a *Miagrope* by Anne Klassen © 1997 by Pembina Threshermans Museum

"Royal Canadian Mounted Police" by Mary Elias © 1997 by Pembina Threshermans Museum

Booze and Prohibition

The 1916 referendum question "Are you in favor of bringing the Manitoba Temperance Act into force?" was answered by a resounding "yes" from 50,484 voters and a "no" from 26,302 voters.

Thereafter, businesses like the Coblentz store in Gretna had its liquor license restricted to selling alcohol for medicinal purposes only. A new business venture in the area was born—bootlegging.

Prohibition and the Border Patrol

Prohibition was enforced in the United States of America, and many Americans did not like it. In order to prevent the smuggling of alcoholic beverages from Canada into the U.S., the Royal Canadian Mounted Police (RCMP) patrolled the Canada – U.S. boundary that extended from the official customs office in Gretna to the official customs office in Emerson. They rode their horses along the roads between the border towns to keep a watchful eye out for illicit trafficking. The RCMP knew that on occasion, some farmers on small farms near the border took economic advantage of America's prohibition.

The farmers knew that the Americans were eager to buy alcoholic beverages in Canada. The Americans crossed the border at a time and place where they hoped no one would see them—especially not the RCMP and the U.S. border patrols. They purchased booze from their Canadian brewing friends and smuggled their purchases back into the States well after the sun had set. The Americans purchased alcoholic beverages for personal consumption and for resale.

They bought booze in the Canadian government stores, and they bought privately. The private purchases were generally from the farmers who the RCMP were watching very carefully. The farmers should not be selling booze. That was illegal. Only government could sell the brew that they made. The farmers, however, saw the American need for alcohol as a golden opportunity to enhance their cashflow. Brewing operations started in numerous households near the border. Although every farmer said the brew was for personal consumption, it was no mystery that they readily exchanged their mash for cash. Even the Mennonite farmers, many of whom frowned on alcohol and alcohol consumption, took advantage of this economic opportunity.

– The names are changed to protect the identity of the brewers.

– Story told to the author by her Aunt Olga Sawatzky, March 25, 2002

The RCMP knew where many of the stills in the districts were located, and they were mighty suspicious that there were more operations than they were aware of. The brewers did their best to hide their operations from the RCMP because they had the authority to put a very sudden stop to their lucrative little industries.

The police on their mounted horses were checking the farms along the border between Emerson and Gretna for brew operations when the Bauenhofens had a mash brewing. The mash was bubbling and gurgling in a large crock in the kitchen. The Bauenhofens saw RCMP approaching their farmhouse and they knew that if the RCMP found their mash, that would mean the end to their monetary relationship with the Americans. They had no place to hide the brewing crock where the RCMP could not or would not look. They had to think of something fast. The RCMP were coming closer. What could they do? After a few short moments of "backing and forthing", they made a decision. They pushed and pulled the heavy stone crock of brewing mash across the wooden floor to rest under a large chair. Mrs. Bauenhofen, who was a woman of considerable size, would sit upon that same chair. She carefully arranged her large, long skirt and sat down on the chair to hide the secret. When the RCMP arrived, Mrs. Bauenhofen did not get up to greet them.

The RCMP knew there was something odd at the Bauenhofen home. The Bauenhofens could hide a crock of brew, but they could not hide its powerful stink. Since they found no visible evidence of a brewing operation, the RCMP had no option but to mount their horses and gallop away. The Bauenhofens continued with their business and were very pleased to see the backsides of the RCMP's horses trotting down their lane.

Bootlegging Challenges

Peter S. and Katharina Hildebrand
|
Katharina Maria Olga Helen Anna Peter Abram Henrietta Henry Eva

During the Prohibition, bootleggers from the United States of America found a path from Canada to the United States directly across Peter S. and Katharina Hildebrand's yard. There was no question about it, the bootleggers would go to almost any length to avoid the U.S. – Canada customs in nearby Emerson or Gretna. They were smuggling booze across the border for a lucrative profit and any custom's officer worth a grain of salt would put an end to a bootlegger's illegal business. Unfortunately for the Americans, the path across the Hildebrand farm was simply a half-mile long farm trail that had been etched out of the land by Peter's farm horses and implements. On their homeward bound trek from Canada to the United States, the bootleggers encountered mud, snowstorms and sleet. They traveled under cover of darkness to avoid being seen by border patrols or the RCMP. It was not unusual for them to get stuck in the sticky black mud and in the deep drifts of prairie snow. In the black of the night, they could not see the mountainous snow drifts or the deep potholes engorged with mud and water.

On nights when the illegal alcohol traffickers got stuck, Peter S. could hear gruff voices talking outside the window of the bedroom that he shared with Katharina. It was an eerie feeling, hearing unfamiliar voices talking outside when he knew that all his family were asleep, and the closest

– Stories told to the author by her Auntie Anne, her Aunt Olga and her Uncle Peter, March 23, 2002.

neighbour was not within earshot. Whenever Peter heard these sounds, he knew someone needed help. He rose from his bed, being careful not to awaken his sleeping wife, put on his hat, and went outdoors to find out what the fellows with the gruff voices needed. The sheepish Americans explained to Peter S. what their dilemma was. They were stuck and needed to get to America before the morning sun exposed them and their illicit cargo.

Peter knew very well that in order for the men not to get caught, they had to get back across the border while it was dark. He also knew that if they did not get across the border before daylight, they would spend another day loafing in his yard, and that did not make his Katharina happy. She was uncomfortable with the loitering strangers who only spoke English and spent too much time chatting with her innocent children. She did not know or trust what those men were saying to her children.

Peter harnessed his horses and helped the Americans' teams get unstuck and on their way back to America. After all, it was the neighbourly thing to do.

"Fun in the Tub" by Mary Elias © 1997 by Pembina Threshermans Museum

Childbirth and Babies

During the late 1800s, many mothers and babies died in childbirth. The young Mennonite mothers mourned for their lost babies. The young fathers mourned for their lost babies and often for their wives who died during childbirth.

The women gave each other spiritual and physical support during the birthing. Catarina Hildebrand (born 1862) had an exceptionally difficult time delivering her babies. When she went into labour, the village women gathered by her bedside to pray for Catarina and her unborn child. She safely delivered seven of her ten children. She could not deliver three of the babies that she had carried for nine months. There were no instruments to help with the delivery. The babies were removed from her womb with sterilized farm implements borrowed from the next door neighbour, Bishop Abraham Doerksen.

Midwifery

Hospitals, doctors, nurses, orderlies, and hospital beds have not always been part of the natural environment in which women have given birth to their babies. Before the 1940s, women used the support of medical professionals very sparingly.

Katharina Hildebrand delivered all her babies in the bedroom that she shared with her husband Peter on their Edenburg farm. At the age of 21, on October 13, 1910, she delivered her first bouncing baby girl, Katharina. Twenty years later, on December 19, 1930 she delivered her last miracle, Eva, in her own cozy maternity ward.

Katharina delivered her babies with a doctor in attendance and her midwife at her side. Her midwife was not really a midwife. She was Aganetha, her sister-in-law, who was a support to Katharina and an assistant to the doctor if necessary. Aganetha lived on the quarter section of land directly east of where Katharina and Peter lived.

When it came time for Katharina to deliver her babies, the doctor was hastily summoned from Gretna. Peter, Katharina's faithful husband, hitched the horses to the buggy and rushed to Gretna to fetch the doctor.

Over the twenty-year span that Katharina gave birth to her ten children, the Gretna doctors who attended to her were Dr. McKenty, Dr. MacKenzie, and Dr. Simpson. As soon as Katharina's husband summoned the doctor, he quickly drove his car to the farm, five miles east of Gretna, and helped deliver the babies. A few days after the delivery, he made a follow-up visit to the farm to check on the well-being of the mother and her new infant.

For their first children, Peter himself had to collect his brother's wife Aganetha to attend the birth. As the first born children grew older, they had to run to their aunt's home with the message *"Daut es Tiet* (It is time)." Aganetha needed no explanation. She knew exactly what those words meant.

Aganetha dropped whatever she was doing, and rushed along the dirt path, hardened by many trips between the two households, to attend to her sister-in-law. Her first task was to empty the

– Told to me by Auntie Anne Schellenberg, May, 1999. Anne's sisters, Olga and Henrietta provided additions and amendments at Anne's home, March 25, 2002.

house of her nervous and anxious brother-in-law Peter, and all his children. She sent them all to her house while she assisted Katharina in delivering the baby.

If the onset of delivery was during the wee hours of the night, Peter woke his children to go to their Aunt Aganetha's home. The children could all sleep on the floor with their cousins. Not one child objected. To have a sleepover was truly a treat, and to sleep on the floor was such fun because it was so out of the ordinary.

When their aunt returned back to her home the next day, she always had news of a new baby that had arrived during the night. The children could not run home fast enough to see the new little person who would be sharing their home.

When it came time for Aganetha to deliver her babies, Katharina assisted Aganetha and Aganetha's children had a sleep-over at Katharina's home.

The women had no training in the art of baby delivery, except for what they had learned from their own mothers, and from their own experiences. It was a time of mutual support and bonding between the women. They were there for each other—for the good times and for the hard times. Together the women rejoiced over the arrival of a healthy infant. Together they wept when the delivery was too complicated or too hard for the baby to survive. The most difficult times were when neither the mother nor the baby survived. Only the midwife and the doctor were there to weep and to take the sad news to the worried husband and his children.

Along with the ten babies that Katharina birthed and raised, she also had two miscarriages. She confided in her daughter-in-law Anna that having the miscarriages had been more difficult than giving birth to her babies. Even though she had experienced birthing so often, she knew the risks of giving birth. When the women helped each other during childbirth, it was always with a prayer in their hearts asking for the safe delivery of mother and child.

Peter's Arrival

Peter S. and **Katharina** Hildebrand
|
Katharina Maria Olga Helen Anna **Peter** Abram Henrietta Henry Eva

On September 3, 1920, their first son finally arrived. Peter S. and Katharina already had five girls and they had waited and waited for a son. There was no question about it—this boy would be named after his father. He would be a Peter too. He would be Peter D. Hildebrand. The "D" represented Katharina's maiden name Doerksen.

It did not matter that Peter was born during harvest season—this was cause for celebration. Peter S. hitched his heavy farm horses to the wooden–wheeled buggy and giddy-upped the horses five miles west towards Gretna to purchase a keg of beer at the Queen's Hotel. There was no time to dilly-dally. It was time to celebrate. The horses and buggy left a cloud of fine harvest dust in their windless wake.

All the way to Gretna, Peter S. Hildebrand's face glowed. Nothing could have made him happier than to become a father of a son. He was so excited, but he knew it was not manly or Mennonite to let his happy excitement show. He wanted to break into song and talk about how joyful his soul felt. He would talk with his Katharina about his joy, but with no one else.

Peter bought the keg of beer at the Queen's hotel and brought it back to the farm to share with his fellow harvesters. There was seldom money to buy such an extravagance, and in truth, it was not the Mennonite way. Many Mennonites frowned upon beer drinking, but Peter threw caution to the wind. He had a baby boy and that was cause for celebration.

Peter tapped the beer keg and filled each harvester's white glass coffee mug with cool frothy beer. What a treat it was. They had few opportunities to enjoy the brew made from the very barley that they grew. They were not accustomed to drinking alcoholic beverages, especially not in the heat of a hot September afternoon and especially not more than a bottle at a time. It took only a little beer for the men to get very drunk. Soon they were stumbling along the stubbled fields and bumping into fence

– On May 29, 1999 this story was told to the author and her mother when they visited the author's Aunt Anne Schellenberg, who had also invited her brother Peter D. and his wife Doris to visit.

posts.   The harvesters were celebrating with abandon, and for the rest of the season, they were the talk of the community when people needed a little chuckle.

Katharina had never seen her husband like this. He was always quiet, and serious. This was totally out of character for him. Many years later, after her baby Peter D. was a husband and a father, Katharina confided in Peter D.'s wife Doris that Peter S. had had so much celebratory beer that day that he had crawled home from the field. Katharina had not said much to her husband at the time. She had just savoured her own little chuckle all by herself.

Harvesters with a keg of beer

Eva's Delivery

Peter S. and **Katharina** Hildebrand   Henry and **Aganetha** Hildebrand
|
Tina Maria **Olga** Helen Anna Peter Abram Henrietta Henry **Eva**

Olga was fourteen years old when her mother, Katharina went into labour with her last baby. Olga had no idea that her mother was going to have a baby. Sure, she had seen that there was a lump under her mother's apron, but perhaps her mother had just been eating too much *Kjielkje* and *Schmaunt Fat* (homemade noodles with cream gravy).

When Katharina's labour pains began, she did not mention it to a soul until the hour of delivery was very near. When that time came, she quietly told her husband *"Nü es daut Tiet* (Now it is time)." Her husband Peter knew from previous births that he had to jump into action immediately. He had to go to town to let the doctor know that his services were immediately required at their farmhouse. He fetched their sister-in-law Aganetha to assist the doctor in the delivery. He rushed his seven children who were still living at home, to Aganetha's house where they would stay until the new infant arrived. Fortunately Aganetha lived only a few paces to the east of Katharina and Peter, so the children could easily walk there. Peter did not tell any of his children, including sixteen–year old Helen and fourteen–year old Olga, why they suddenly all had to visit their Aunt Aganetha.

On December 9, 1930, Olga did not want to go to her aunt's home when Peter suddenly directed all his children to go there without any apparent reason. Olga wanted to stay home with her mother, but Katharina insisted that Olga go to her Aunt Aganetha's house. It was not like Katharina to be so insistent. Usually when Olga wanted to do something, Katharina consented, but this time was different. Reluctantly Olga shuffled to her aunt's house. She could not figure out why her mother was behaving so oddly and why she had to go to her aunt's house when her aunt went to her house.

Later that day Aganetha returned to her own home. Her house was bustling with all her children and all of Katharina and Peter's children. Aganetha was tired from helping her sister-in-law Katharina deliver her last baby, and she wasted no time directing Olga and all her siblings, "*Nü kjenn jie aula no Hüs gone* (Now you can all go home)." The children walked home, only to learn that while they had been away, a brand new pink baby had arrived at their home. Olga puzzled, how could this be? Why did their babies always arrive when Olga's mother and father were at home but all their children were away? By the time the children arrived home, Olga's mother and father had already chosen a name for the baby girl. Her name would be Eva. Olga took a close look at her baby sister nursing at her mother's breast. Her first question to her mother was why the baby had a red mark on her forehead. Katharina didn't miss a beat. She explained to her fourteen-year-old daughter that the baby had got the mark from the suitcase in which the stork had delivered baby Eva. The suitcase had been too small for the baby.

Olga accepted that answer. Eva grew up with the mark from the stork's suitcase. It always appeared when she was excited—a reminder of where she had come from!

"Recess Time" by Mary Elias © 1997 by Pembina Threshermans Museum

Live and Learn

School means a whole lot more than reading, 'riting, and 'rithmetic. Learning means a whole lot more than school.

Children grew up hearing little sayings that their parents repeated over the years. Helena Sawatzky often said to her children:

"*Was ich selber tu, trau ich noch ein andern zu.*" (What I do myself, I also trust others to do.)

"If you ever have to move because of your neighbours, make sure your neighbours do not move with you."

"It is best if parents and their children cannot see the smoke from each other's chimneys."

When her children were too concerned about appearances, Katharina Hildebrand often said:

"*Wäa doa sacht foat, dee jleewt daut mott so. Wäa doa stoak foat, dee sit daut nijch.*"
(Who drives slowly, believes it should be that way. Who drives fast, does not see it.)

Getting Ready for School

– Told to the author by her Aunt Olga Sawatzky

Peter S. and **Katharina** Hildebrand
|
Katharina Maria Olga Helen Anna Peter Abram Henrietta Henry Eva

Katharina liked pretty things, and she took care that her belongings always looked neat and tidy. As a young mother, she liked nothing better than to have her five young girls Katharina, Mary, Helen, Olga, and Anna look pretty, neat, and tidy. Katharina and Peter did not have any cash to buy pretty things, but every morning before school, Katharina checked her little girls' hair ribbons. If they were wrinkled, she heated her sad irons on the kitchen stove and ironed the ribbons as flat as the prairie horizon, and then she braided each little girl's hair. Katharina wove the ribbon into the braids and tied the end of the braid with a crisp bow. She made each of her daughters two French braids that started at the forehead and ran the length of the hair. The girls looked ever so pristine and pressed when they left the farmhouse on their two–mile walk to school. Each girl carried her lunch in a syrup pail. Katharina had packed them a lunch of her homemade bread, spread with Edenburg Syrup that Peter had bought at Kaufmanns's Store in Gretna. Syrup was one of the few things Katharina did not make at home.

It did not matter that by the time lunch rolled around at school, the syrup sandwiches were stiff as shoe leather. The girls with the pretty ribbons in their hair were hungry and they ate their sandwiches with gusto, just like all the other children who ate their syrup or lard sandwiches.

– Sad irons were oval shaped metal irons heated on the stove. A detachable handle held the iron in place for ironing. When the iron got too cool for ironing, it was returned to the stove for reheating and the handle was attached to another iron heating on the stove. Sad irons predated electric irons.

The Educator

Peter S. and Katharina Hildebrand
|
Katharina **Maria** Helen Olga Anna Peter Abram Henrietta Henry Eva

Maria was a thespian with a mission. As a young teenager, she worked for the Doerksen family. Along with her many tasks of cooking, cleaning, gardening, mending, milking the cows, and slopping the hogs, she also had the duty of minding the children. Actually, her task was to mind the little Doerksen boys. The very words "the Doerksen boys" could put the fear of the Lord into any would-be childcare worker.

Maria had just finished dusting the potatoes with Paris Green, a powder intended to terminate pesky potato beetles that dared to munch on her potato crop. It was her duty to ensure that the children were safe and did not eat any of the pretty green poisonous powder.

Maria pulled up all her dramatic skills and provided the rowdy little boys with an object lesson to be remembered. She called them to her side and in her most teacher-like voice, said, "*Junges, wan jie dit äte, dan woa jie stoawe* (Boys, if you eat this, then you will die)." She slowly brushed her pointing finger against the green powder and brought it to her mouth, pretending to lick her powdered finger. Maria tumbled to the ground in mock spasms of pain and anguish. She lay still as a snowflake on a frozen blade of grass. In her mind, the boys should have been shocked out of their dirty little socks with the holes in them. They should have been trying to roust her petite body from the dead. They should have been weeping, gnashing their teeth, and asking Maria's still body for forgiveness for all their transgressions. None of that happened.

Not to be outsmarted by Maria, one of the little cherubs slowly unbuckled his belt and slipped it from the two remaining trouser loops of his faded hand-me-down pants. He raised the belt high into the air and lashed it down on Maria's prone body. Maria arose from her "death" like lightening. Her little charges pointed their grubby fingers at her as they doubled over with spasms of laughter.

Maria knew she had to rethink her teaching methods.

St. Vitus Dance

Peter S. and Katharina Hildebrand
|
Katharina Mary **Olga Helen** Anna Peter Abram Henrietta Henry Eva

St. Vitus Dance: a childhood movement disorder characterized by rapid irregular, aimless, involuntary movements of the muscles, of the limbs, face and trunk. The onset is typically between the ages of 5 and 15. It often occurs after rheumatic fever. A complete recovery usually occurs. The average case lasts 3-6 weeks.

Helen was a young schoolgirl when diagnosed with *Feitsdauns* (St. Vitus Dance). The doctor advised Helen's parents, Katharina and Peter, to "take it easy on her," and not to place too many demands on her. Peter asked the teacher to also follow the doctor's recommendation at school. He quietly asked the teacher that he not put too many expectations on his Helen at school.

Helen was a prankster. She saw her diagnosis as a rich opportunity to create a little fun at school without having to face any punitive action—after all, the teacher was to "take it easy" on her.

Her school desk was the very last desk in a row of six desks. The desktops and the seats were screwed to two long planks on the floor. Each varnished seat and desktop, with the hole for the ink well, accommodated two students.

All the children were seated at their desks and listening to their teacher. That is, all the children except Helen. Helen tapped her desk mate on the shoulder and held her pointing finger to her lips, cautioning her desk mate to remain quiet. She wiggled out of her seat, onto the floor under her

– Story told to the author by her Aunt Olga on October 26, 2002.

desk, got down on her tummy, and slowly crept under the seats occupied by the children in front of her. She slithered forward like a clumsy snake until she came to her sister Olga's seat.

From Helen's flat-on-her-belly point of view under the seats, all she could see were children's woolen stockings and their heavy, scuffed shoes. Some shoes had signs of visiting the barn before school that morning. Helen recognized her sister Olga's hand-me-down shoes and thick stockings. She stopped and tickled Olga's legs. Then she tickled Olga's desk mate's legs as lightly as a dusting feather.

Olga and her desk mate could not help themselves. They covered their mouths with their hands to keep their giggles from coming out. Then the snickering and giggling spread to all the other students in the one-room schoolhouse. They too covered their mouths and kept their giggles in their stomachs. They did not want the teacher to discover Helen out of her seat. Quiet as the stuffed owl in the corner of the room, Helen crawled backwards, retracing her route under and between the children's legs. She wiggled her way backwards into her desk without the teacher noticing that she had ever left.

She was as innocent as apple pie without cinnamon.

Peanut Butter Sandwiches

Peter S. and Katharina Hildebrand
|
Katharina Maria **Helen** Olga Anna Peter Abram Henrietta Henry Eva

Helen knew what peanuts were. Every Christmas they sold peanuts in huge gunny sacks at Nitikman Bros. in Gretna. Helen had never heard of peanut butter sandwiches though. The only sandwiches that were ever in her lunch pail were the syrup sandwiches, jam sandwiches, lard sandwiches, and the occasional bologna sandwiches that were oh, so special.

Helen was curious about the lunches the other children ate from their recycled syrup pails that served as lunch kits. Some children's sandwiches were big, some were small, some were floppy, and some looked a little like the cardboard with that funny ribbing between the layers. Helen was particularly interested in the Loeppky children's sandwiches. They had peanut butter sandwiches. She had seen one of the Loeppky children take a bite of her peanut butter sandwich during the morning recess, and then put it back in her syrup pail so that she had something left to eat at her noon meal. Helen wanted to taste that sandwich. When the Loeppky kid was out of sight, and no big kids were watching her, she peeked into that lunch pail and feasted her eyes on a peanut butter sandwich. Helen could not stop herself. She had to take the sandwich. It was tempting her like the apple tempted Adam. She took a bite. It was delicious. Helen could not stop at one bite. She ate the whole thing, and the poor little Loeppky girl had none.

Besides having a curiosity about what other children ate, Helen was also interested in what they drank. She and her brothers and sisters took bottles of *Prips* (coffee substitute from cereal grain) to school. They filled empty bottles from Wonder Oil, vanilla and *Alpenkräuter* (herbal alcoholic beverage) with their *Prips*. All the other kids in school used recycled bottles to hold their beverages too. Most of the kids took *Prips* to school, but Helen knew that little Jeanne Schmidt had real coffee with real cream in her *Alpenkräuter* bottle. Helen wanted Jeanne's real coffee. One morning Helen secretly opened Jeanne's lunch pail and spirited away her *Alpenkräuter* bottle filled with coffee. Little Jeanne saw Helen just as she whisked away with the bottle. Jeanne chased after that naughty Helen, and shouted at her to give back her coffee. Helen was smaller and friskier than Jeanne was. Jeanne could not catch her. With Jeanne's bottle in hand, Helen kept out of Jeanne's reach as she sipped the delicious dark brown coffee, with a touch of cream—just the way Helen liked it.

School Yard Competition

Johan M. and Helena Sawatzky
|
Tina Nettie Heinrich Jakob Helen Mary Marge Anna John **Diedrich** Willie

"Boys will be boys," was the way the saying went. Diedrich was a boy and like many little boys, his humour was bathroom humour. Diedrich and his little friends all went to the same Blumenthal School and at recess they played in the playground, surrounded by trees on three sides.

During recess all the children played organized games. They played baseball, Anti-Anti Over, and Kick the Can. However, on occasion, the small children wandered off and played without the big kids. They played their own games and made up their own competitions. They were all boys, except for that girl Mary who always wanted to play with the boys.

The little boys designed a competition. The object of the competition was to pee the longest distance. The rule required that they all had to stand in a straight line, and then pee as far as they could. The child who peed the farthest won. The boys were all lined up and ready to start the competition without Mary. They had not included Mary in their plans, but she insisted that she should be in the competition. Diedrich and his little buddies thought this was very silly, because Mary didn't have a chance of beating any boy in this competition. The boys humoured her. They consented to let Mary get in the line and compete with them.

They were all ready to start the competition when Mary added one extra rule. "*Kjeina kaun de Henj brucke* (No one could use his hands)." They all stood in a row ready for the competition. The moment the competition began, Mary added another twist. She squatted and won "hands down".

– Story told to the author by her father, Henry D. Hildebrand at a Thanksgiving gathering, October 13, 2001.

– The girl's name has been changed to Mary to protect the identity of the real person.

Sketch by Katie Altendorf Cable © 2003

Thanks to Jake Neufeld

– Story told to the author by her Uncle John Sawatzky, July 14, 2001.

Johan M. and Helena Sawatzky
|
Tina Nettie Heinrich Jakob Helen Mary Marge Anna **John** Diedrich Willie

John struggled in school. It wasn't because he was a dull student. He was a fine student, but in the fall of each year, when all the other students returned to school after the summer holidays, John stayed away. He had to help with the harvest and the fieldwork on the farm. His father got special permission from the Department of Education, allowing John to return to school six weeks after all the other students followed September's beckoning ring of the teacher's school bell. John could catch up with the other children when he finally did return to school, but he needed help. Help came from his special friend, Jake Neufeld. Jake was a math whiz, and after school, he brought his buddy John up to speed with all the other kids.

Mr. Bock, the Blumenthal schoolteacher, had no time to give John additional help. Mr. Bock had seventy children from grade one to grade eight under his tutelage. Some years he had additional students taking high school education by correspondence in his class as well. John's education was definitely not a special priority for Mr. Bock.

Nevertheless, John persevered despite his teacher and despite his late school entry. By spring, John finally felt as though he had caught up with his classmates. But every spring, his father again got permission from the Department of Education to have his young son exempted from school attendance so that John could help put the crop in. John obliged. He missed another six weeks of school. Again he turned to his friend Jake Neufeld for help. It was a struggle for John. He had just caught up with his work, and now he had to be out of school again—just before the final exams.

The final exams counted for a lot. Sometimes the Christmas and Easter exams made up part of the final mark, but as often as not, John had all 100 percent riding on that final exam in each subject. John passed and he gave the credit to his friend Jake.

John became a life-long learner—a credit to a young friend who made all the difference.

Fun and Games

"We played and played. We played indoors and outdoors. We pretended that we were mothers and fathers, and we pretended that we were babies.

I was fourteen when my mother said to my sisters and me, 'Girls, it is time to put away your dolls.' I was not ready to put my dolls away."

Olga Hildebrand Sawatzky
November, 2002

Rain Song

A song sung by children when it rained…

Es regnet auf die Brücke	It's raining on the bridge
Und ich werde nasz	And I am getting wet
Ich habe was vergessen	I have forgotten something
Und weisz nicht was	And I don't know what
Liebe Linde jung und frei	Dear Linde young and free
Komm mit mir zum Tanz herein	Come with me to the dance inside
Komm, wir wollen tanzen	Come, we want to dance
Und lustig sein.	And be happy.

– On August 15, 2001, when the author along with relatives visited her Aunt Anne Schellenberg in Altona, Anne and her sister Henrietta broke into song—Rain Song—when the weather was discussed.

Katharina's Polka

Abraham and Maria Doerksen
|
Katharina and Peter S. Hildebrand

Red-haired Katharina was Abraham and Maria Doerksen's first daughter. Katharina was born in the village of Sommerfeld, where her parents had settled in the late 1800s after they had left their home in Russia (Ukraine) near the Sea of Azov. Her father called her by her Christian name, Katharina. Everyone else called her *Trientji*.

Katharina's growing up years in Sommerfeld were rich with girlfriends, work, family and play. She loved to spend glorious days with her village girlfriends and, whenever possible, Katharina avoided working on her own. She much preferred to work and play with someone. It was so much better to herd cows or pick string beans with her girlfriend next door or with her sister than to do it all by herself. When she grew older, those gentle days were memories mirrored in rainbows.

Many years later, after Katharina had raised her own children to adulthood, she delighted in telling her grandchildren about her childhood days in Sommerfeld. A favourite memory of hers was one of summer Sunday evenings in the village. After the cows had been milked, the chickens given their rations of grain, and the hogs served generous portions of *Schroot* (chopped grain) soaked in water, it was time for fun.

Katharina's blonde-braided village girlfriends gathered on the road guarded by regiments of poplar trees on either side. The girls knew that Katharina would come armed with harmonica in hand and would be ready to play lively polkas for them to dance to. Katharina stood just outside the circle of girls, brought her harmonica to her mouth, and played one spirited polka after another. Her one bare foot in her worn leather shoe started to tap while the other foot kept still. Her brilliant red hair resisted the constraints of her tight braids. As she bounced to the music, her tucked-in tendrils peeked out to frame her joyful face.

It took no time at all before the girls in their long cotton dresses were kicking up their heels and swinging each other round and round. They danced with their whole beings until after the sun set and they could hardly see each other in the darkening evening.

Katharina's father brought the girls back to village reality. His deep voice boomed from the Doerksen doorway, "*Mejales, daut es nü Tiet no Hüs to gone* (Girls, now it is time to go home)." Katharina's harmonica stopped mid-note as if it too had understood the order from her father. The girls' dancing halted mid-swing. They had all heard the call and knew they had to obey Katharina's father.

His words were heeded, not only because he was Katharina's father, but also because he was the bishop of the church.

The girls hastily bid each other adieu, knowing they would see each other throughout the week, but there was just a little sadness, knowing that yet another Sunday evening had come to an end. They would not dance to Katharina's harmonica for another whole week—not until the next Sunday.

Homemade Parties

- Story told to the author by her Aunt Olga, October 26, 2002.

Peter S. and **Katharina** Hildebrand
|
Katharina Maria Helen Olga Anna Peter Abram Henrietta Henry Eva

Katharina and Peter both played the accordion and the harmonica. Katharina especially loved to play lively tunes on her harmonica. But she would just as eagerly dance to the polkas that Peter squeezed out on his accordian. After supper and the day's work was done, Peter picked up the accordion to play for his own enjoyment and his family's entertainment. As soon as he started to play, Katharina's toe began to tap and her hands clapped in time to the music. She could not sit still with her crochet hooks and knitting needles. She called her little girls, "*Kommt Mejales. Well wie daunse* (Come girls. Let's dance)." Quick as lightning, she was on the floor dancing around the kitchen table with her five little girls, Tina, Maria, Helen, Olga, and Anna.

The little girls loved it best when their father played a spirited rendition of *De Ül de schit von Boom herauf* (The owl poops down from

Katharina's dance partners:
Katharina, Maria, Helen, Olga,
Peter, Anna, Abram

the tree). The girls in their faded and patched cotton dresses danced in squares and swung in circles. Katharina taught her girls to square dance, waltz, polka, and foxtrot. She even taught them Heel Toe—Here We Go. Katharina and her five cherubs filled the kitchen "dance floor". It did not matter that their scuffed shoes had soles worn to paper thickness. It did not matter that their legs had got longer and their dresses had not grown to keep pace with the growing legs. They were having the time of their life, dancing the early evening away. The dance floor was full with Katharina and her girls. When the little boys, Peter and Abram, cut in, nobody minded. There was always room for one more dancer on the floor when the music was playing.

The times were tough, but it was not all drought and grasshoppers.

Helen

Peter S. and Katharina Hildebrand
|
Katharina Maria **Helen** Olga Anna Peter Abram Henrietta Henry Eva

Helen was the third daughter in the family. The boys and more girls came later. Helen was a gifted storyteller and a practical joker. Her parents, Katharina and Peter tried hard to determine in which gene pool those characteristics had been hatched. After all, both Peter and Katharina were very serious and hard-working individuals, although Katharina did have her own penchant for humour and mischief making. As a youth, she had been the harmonica playing, dance-calling girl in the village of Sommerfeld when the village girls gathered for their lively Sunday evening get-togethers.

Whether it was the *Jugendverein* (Youth Group), the local Co-Op talent program, or the Christmas concert in the one-room school house, Helen contributed her keen visual, and sometimes caustic humour for all to enjoy. Her father Peter dreaded his daughter's productions because he felt certain that she would embarrass him. She lived up to his expectations. She embarrassed him. Peter much preferred to go through life without fanfare. As the

sedate head of the family, he did not suffer humour at his expense well—especially when it came from his own exuberant offspring.

On one such public occasion, Helen did not partake in the usual drama and poetry performances. She sat quietly by. This in itself was enough of an anomaly for her father to raise his antennae and be on the alert for a crisis. It was a Christmas party and gifts would be exchanged. At home there had been no family huddles discussing gifts, but there was suspicion that Helen might have anonymously placed a few articles under the decorated tree.

The gifts were distributed. Mostly they were the usual handkerchiefs, skeins of embroidery cotton, or a flowered china cup and saucer. One of the gifts, covered with wax paper, was unceremoniously unwrapped and much to the surprise of the recipient, the gift was the snout of a hog that had met its demise on the slaughter floor a month earlier. Helen had assisted at the annual fall hog butchering bee, and had squirreled away the snout

– Helen's poem was recited to the author by her Aunt Olga Sawatzky (born 1915) on August 3, 2000.

---

in a cool November porch. It wasn't enough for her to present only the snout, but couched inside each nostril she had cleverly inserted a green candy.

Imagine the response. Who gave this gift? The unsharpened lead pencil greeting on the waxed paper had only identified who the gift was for, and not whom the gift was from.

Unlike terrorists claimng responsibility for their acts, no one claimed responsibility for this breach of decorum. No one asked anyone specifically *"Deidst dü daut* (Did you do that)?" Helen was quiet. Her father was quiet too, but he wondered if the culprit might be eating and sleeping under his very own roof. No one said a word.

When the family got home from the festivities, Peter, knowing of his daughter's leaning towards humour that occasionally lacked in good taste, asked, *"Lensch, gaufst dü irjent wäm fonndoage en Wienachts Jeschenkj* (Helen, did you give anyone Christmas presents today)?"

"Blooss miene Frind (Only my friends)," she replied. She kept busy embroidering the red rose on the pillowcase, not allowing her eyes to stray. Peter went back to reading the "Steinbach Post", rustling it purposefully so that Helen couldn't hear his little snicker. He didn't pursue any questions about a second gift of Lifebuoy soap. That gift had suspiciously also had only the pencilled name of the recipient, written on its brown paper wrapping. The recipient was a young man with very significant body odour. Once again, the giver remained anonymous.

Like her mother, Helen was creative with words. She wrote and presented poems and drama at local functions. She had no regard for editing or for political correctness. What she wrote, she presented.

On one such occasion at the Farmers Union of Manitoba meeting, Helen presented a poem of her creation. The Farmers Union Meeting was an occasion for the whole community. It was not

Helen

a meeting with just the usual annual reports, words from the president or the treasurer, and motions to be passed. No, this was a community event with speeches by Dave and William Heinrichs and with the all-important local talent show.

Helen saw this as her opportunity to showcase her comedic talent. She wrote her own poems and recited them for a full house of local folks—from babes-in-arms, to gangly teenagers to gray haired seniors with canes. Her poetry was an instant hit. She struck such a cord with Mr. Daniel Heinrichs that the portly gentleman laughed so hard, he fell off his chair.

The community's first language was *Plautdietsch*, and so was Helen's poetry. Helen approached the podium, cleared her throat, looked around the room, and recited her poetry with pride and dignity. No one, especially her father, doubted that it was an original poem by the one and only Helen Hildebrand.

Dan ha ejk noch ein Schwoaga	Then I also have a brother-in-law
De wea sea maoga	He is very skinny
Forakje en de Schwoaga schmäkje	Father and the brother-in-law smoke
Daut mo jrod so tum fläkje	It's enough to swear
De Schwoaga haft twee Kjinja	The brother-in-law has two children
Daut senn mo kjleene Dinkja	They are just little things
Murakje spoat de Eia toop	Mother saves the eggs together
See well doa fea en niea Hoot	She wants from them a new hat
Furakje sajt ejk well Tobback han	Father says I want to have tobacco
Nämt de Eia en foat no Nitigmann*	Take the eggs and drive to Nitigmann*
Dan ha wie noch sass Pead	Then we also have six horses
De stone uck aula enna Räj	They also all stand in a row
En dan kjemmt daut kjleene wittet Kaulf	And then comes that little white calf
En jnajt de Kjäj de Tsägel auf	And nibbles the cow's tail off
Dan ha wie uck noch fief Heena	Then we also have five hens
De läve direkt von Speena	They live directly on shavings

Helen as a youth

Helen's father was apoplectic. In a small community,
it was hard to pretend she was someone else's child.

Anna Learns to Ride a Bike

Johan M. and Helena Sawatzky
|
Tina Netttie Heinrich Jakob Helen Mary Marge **Anna** John Diedrich Willie

Anna was determined. She would learn to ride that two-wheeled bicycle no matter what. She walked the bike to the top of one of the hills beside the pond in the cow pasture. There was a hill on each side of the pond. The hills were piles of dirt that had been dug to make the deep pond.

Anna firmly grasped the handlebars with her little hands and then she swung her chubby leg over the seat of the bike and quickly placed her foot on the bicycle pedal. Fast as she could, she put her other foot, the one that had been holding her upright, on the other pedal. The bike edged forward and downward. Anna held on for her dear little life.

Her body was as rigid as the gate post at the end of their driveway. The spotted cows in the pasture watched with slight amusement as the determined little girl sped down the hill.

When she got to the bottom of the hill, Anna made her little legs move the pedals of the bike round and round. She wanted to keep the bicycle from falling over for as long as she could. Soon the bike started to lean too far to the left and then too far to the right. Anna had to make a choice. She could fall and end up with scraped body parts, or she could put one foot on the ground and try to steady herself. Then, on the other hand, she

– Story told to the author by her mother, Anna Sawatzky Hildebrand, May 13, 2001.

could put both her feet on the ground and catapult forward like a rocket as the pedals slammed against the back of her legs. Anna fell.

She tried again. She walked the bike up the hill. She mounted the bike. She put her feet back on the pedals. The bike edged forward and down the hill. Anna pedaled, and down she went, hitting the grassy pasture at full speed.

She tried again. She pedaled a few feet without falling. She stayed upright. She was riding a bike. Steady, s-t-e-a-d-y. Anna was oh, so proud, riding a bike all by herself. Oh, oh, there was a cow directly in front of her. It would have to move because Anna had not yet learned to make a turn with her bike. The cow should move really fast.

The cow did not move. Down went Anna. She hit the dirt again. She would have to master the fine art of turning corners so that she could dodge cows, cow pies, fences, and gopher holes. Anna decided she would practice corner turning in the pasture because if she fell, the landing in the pasture was much softer than landing on their gravel yard with the fist-sized stones. Grass and cow pies would stain her clothes, but a gravel fall really hurt.

Drawing of a Threshing Machine by John Wiebe © 1997 by Pembina Threshermans Museum

Farm Work and Farm Animals

Farm life was a way of life, separate from the town and city experience. Farmers and their families were self-sufficient. They repaired their own machinery, they built much of their own machinery, and they provided for their own livestock. When a farmer did not have the skills to perform tasks that needed to be done, he would ask his neighbour for help rather than hire professional help. That was the way things were done.

Gathering Winter Fuel

Johan M. and Helena Sawatzky
|
Tina Nettie **Heinrich** Jakob Helen Mary Marge Anna John Diedrich Willie

---

Johan and his son Heinrich gathered wood for fuel. Firewood was not a readily available commodity on the Blumenthal farm. Every tree growing on the yard had been carefully planted by hand to offer shade and shelter for years to come. The hand-planted trees were not for cutting down to offer a few moments of warmth on a cold winter's night.

Nonetheless, the family needed firewood for the cookstove that cooked all their meals. They needed firewood to heat the bake oven to bake the delicious crusty homemade breads and cakes. They needed firewood to supplement the coal supply so that the family would be toasty warm during the long icy prairie winter with its howling winds and blowing snow.

Before breakfast, during the cold of winter, Johan and his oldest son Heinrich hitched the big workhorses to the wooden sledded stoneboat. Then Johan would say to his boy, "*Jung, well wie noch schwind Freestikj äte, onn dan senn wie unja Wäajes* (Boy, let's quickly eat breakfast, and then we are on our way)."

They slurped their boiled coffee served with thick cream from the cows they had milked the night before, and munched on fat slices of homemade bread slathered with freshly churned butter and preserved rhubarb jam. They were in a hurry, so they did not wait for the girls to fry eggs and *Jreeve* (cracklings) for their breakfast.

On their way out the door to the stoneboat hitched to the horse, Helena reminded her husband, "*Na Papa, feyäte nijch jün Meddach* (Well father, don't forget your dinner)." Their girls, Nettie and Tina had packed them a hearty lunch in a stone crock.

The crock was filled with fried smoked sausage from their very own hogs, slices of pie made from the plum jam they had preserved the previous fall, and buns that had been baked on Saturday.

One last time before the father and son headed out for a day's wood cutting, they checked to make sure they had all their supplies for the day. They were on their way to the wooded banks of the Red River near Dominion City to cut wood for their heating and cooking fuel. The horses pulled the stoneboat along the road over the light snowdrifts to Letellier where they crossed the frozen Red River. It took two hours to get to their destination. The horses were weary. The father and son had a day's work ahead of them.

Each man knew what his job was. Heinrich gripped the axe and chopped the biggest trees. Johan fished the old saw out of the stoneboat and sawed the felled trees into manageable logs that he could hoist into the stoneboat.

The hard work kept the cold from their bones. They didn't talk much. During the day, they met other fathers and sons. They exchanged brief greetings, but there wasn't time for chatter. It was cold and they had a lot of chopping and sawing to do before the sun set. There was still a two-hour ride home in a stoneboat loaded to the hilt with cut lumber. They only hoped the girls had already milked the cows by the time they got there.

Bolting Buckskins

Johan M. and Helena Sawatzky
|
Tina Nettie **Heinrich Jakob** Helen Mary Marge Anna Diedrich John Willie

It was 1935 or 1936. The Sawatzkys had a pair of buckskin-coloured horses. Jess, the mare, and her son Shorty both had a black stripe running along their backs. Johan M. Sawatzky bought Jess at an auction sale. She had been brought to Manitoba from Alberta. She wore a "J" brand, reminding her of the ranch she had come from. Jess was a bronco and like many farmers, Johan bought her because broncos were cheap.

On a cold day in early spring, Jess gave birth to a set of twins in the open field where she could not protect her young ones from the elements or from the other horses. By the time Johan knew that Jess had given birth, the other horses had already killed one of her twins.

Johan took the remaining twin into the house. The children named him Shorty. Shorty was kept in the house behind the stove to keep him warm. Although the small farmhouse was crowded with all the Sawatzky children, they all loved to see the gangly colt take his wobbly steps in their kitchen. They spoiled him with treats. They put no restrictions on him. Shorty could do whatever he pleased and soon Shorty developed an attitude. It was very clear to Shorty that he could call the shots in the Sawatzky kitchen.

When Shorty grew old enough to work, he decided the terms of his employment. When he wanted to rest from pulling a plough, he pretended that he needed to pee. Work was stopped for a moment to give Shorty time to relieve himself, but Shorty did not pee. When he was directed to go back to work, he lay down right in the field. He seemed to be very tired. Since he was still a bit of a spoiled child, another horse was hitched to the plough so that Shorty could rest. At the end of the day, when it was time for the workers and the horses to go home, Shorty had all the energy in the world and raced home as fast as his bronco legs could go.

It seems that Shorty came by his personality quite honestly. His mother, Jess, had some similar characteristics. They were both willful and determined. As Shorty grew up, he and his mother became quite a pair. The two of them were not the kind of horses who were inclined to listen to directions from their humans. If they followed any directions at all, they were directions that came from someone who was strong and bold. Without constant human prompting and reminders, the two horses took matters into their own hands—or own hooves, as it were. They galloped wherever they pleased and at the speed that pleased them.

One day Heinrich and Jakob Sawatzky, Johan's two eldest sons, had the two buckskin horses hitched to the cultivator. Johan had instructed his sons to cultivate the eighty acres behind the Bernhard Neufeld farm, a half-mile east of the Sawatzky home.

When the boys finished cultivating the eighty acres, it was time to go home to feed the hungry animals and to have their own evening meal. During the day, it had gotten so warm that Heinrich had removed his jacket and hung it on the fence post. At the end of the day, he really did not feel like walking the distance to get his jacket, so he ordered his younger brother to get it for him. Jakob had no more energy than Heinrich did.

Jakob did many things for Heinrich, but he did not want to get Heinrich's jacket. He knew that Heinrich just wanted to light up another cigarette before he got home. Jakob boldly told his brother "*Go hol daut selfst* (Go get it yourself)." Heinrich looked at Jakob as if to say, "you asked for it", but he sauntered along the grooved field to get his jacket. Over his shoulder, he muttered to his brother "*Na jo dan, oba wan de Pead wajch ranne, dan es daut diene Schult* (Okay, but if the horses run away, it will be your fault)."

Heinrich fetched his jacket. As he was returning to the cultivator connected to the horses, the horses began to walk. Shorty had managed to get his bridle off, but there was still a rope connecting him to Jess. Heinrich could already see what was going to happen. He raced towards the horses and

– Part of this story was sent in a letter to the author from her Uncle Jakob Sawatzky in January 2002. Part of the story was told to the author by her Uncle John Sawatzky in March 2003.

just barely got onto the cultivator before the horses started to run at top speed.

Jakob watched from a distance. He could only see Heinrich from the rear. Heinrich, a portly fellow, had chubby rear cheeks that jiggled like jelly as he rattled along on the cultivator behind the racing pair of broncos. Jakob howled. This was the funniest sight he had seen in a long time.

Jakob did not laugh for long. Fear and worry soon took over. He could see Heinrich struggle to rein in the horses. They were totally out of control. The horses ran at a full gallop, toward home with the cultivator and Heinrich clattering behind them. As the horses passed a small house on the yard, Shorty stumbled and fell and the cultivator hooked onto the corner of the house. Everything stopped instantly.

Far behind, and as fast as his legs could carry him, Jakob followed the horses, the brother and the cultivator. By the time Jakob got home, Heinrich had blamed the entire incident on his brother because Jakob had laughed at his bouncing cheeks when the incident first started.

Jakob, on the other hand, thought the incident had occurred because the young horse had removed his bridle. Their father informed them that if the rope pulling Shorty had broken, the cultivator shovels would have pierced the dragging young horse. Lucky for Jakob and Heinrich that did not happen. All were safe, including the horses.

John and the Bolting Buckskins

Johan M. and Helena Sawatzky
|
Tina Nettie Heinrich **Jakob** Helen Mary Marge Anna **John** Diedrich Willie

In June, 2001, John Sawatzky wrote about a moment in his childhood:

"My sister Marge and I worked on the field, plowing with four horses each. One day, when I was only nine years old, I was working on the field with the horses and the horses got spooked. They ran away with the rake and with me on it. It was impossible for me to stop them. They ran home and as they were running, the rake caught the corner of the shed and I was thrown off the rake. This resulted in a broken arm and knocking me out."

John's older brother Jakob saw it all happen. When Jakob saw his little brother lying on the ground, he knew for sure that the boy was dead. He was not moving. Jakob was sure that little John would never breathe another breath, but before Jakob could truly understand what had just happened, and what to do with his brother lying lifeless on the ground, little John opened his eyes. Joy and relief washed over Jakob's whole body, when he saw that his precious brother was alive. Little John looked around, trying to remember where he was and why he was on the ground, and why did his big brother Jakob look like he was crying?

Jakob felt so responsible for what had happened. He took all the blame because after all, he had been the one who hitched up the horses for his brother and sister when they went out to plough the field.

Two of the horses that Jakob had hitched up for John were buckskin coloured with a black stripe along the back. They were fine looking horses, but they were not a co-operative team. One was a three-year-old name Shorty and the other was his mother named Jess. Jakob never could figure out what went on in their horse brains the day they bolted with that little boy on the rake. Were they trying to have some fun, or were they taking advantage of an inexperienced "farmer"?

Henrietta's Stooks

Peter S. and Katharina Hildebrand

|

Katharina Maria Olga Helen Anna **Peter** Abram **Henrietta Henry** Eva

The August sun had been blazing for days, and there hadn't been a cloud on the horizon to shower the thirsty cracked fields in weeks. The sun had baked the grey chaff-covered fields to a dry mosaic. The girls in their calf-length homemade skirts and elbow-length men's shirts were perspiring from the heat of the burning sun, and their whole bodies were itching from the prickly oat chaff. The tied sheaths of oats that they were handling had to be set into hour-glass shaped stooks to expose all the grain kernels to the drying sun. The stooks needed to be strong enough to stay upright despite the tireless, relentless prairie winds. Henrietta took it as a personal affront if her stooks succumbed to the gale wind forces. Certainly, she also took full credit when her stooks presented as the driest oat stooks fed to the threshing machine. The threshing machine did a miserable job of threshing poorly set stooks that did not dry properly because their high moisture content caused the stooks to be tough and plug up the machine.

The young boys worked hard on the farm too, but they were delighted to embrace any moments of levity that might be available to them. This was especially true of Henrietta's pesky younger brother Henry and his favourite friend Peter. Peter was also their cousin, and that meant that Henry and Peter could annoy Henrietta and their other sisters all week long and at family gatherings too. On this particular hot day, the two little hayseeds agreed that the best way to make a good joke was to tease Henrietta. They knew exactly what to do to rile her, and they knew exactly what she would do when she got riled. When Henrietta was upset by the boys, she chased them around the dry stubbled field, trying to catch them. This was great fun for the boys because they could easily outrun her. The funniest part was when they almost let her catch up with them, and then quick as the striped gophers on the field, they scampered away.

The boys had a plan. Quietly, in the lull of the still, stifling afternoon, they tiptoed by a stook that Henrietta had just set up into a perfect teepee shape. They held their forefingers to their pursed

Sketch by Katie Altendorf Cable © 2003

lips in mock sincerity and whispered, just loud enough for Henrietta to hear, "Shhhhhhh, be quiet when you are close to Henrietta's stooks or they will fall apart." How dare those two rascals insult her workmanship? The boys knew their insult would give chase. Quickly as a mouse running away from the claws of a cat, the boys dashed from the reach of Henrietta's hands. It was lucky for the boys that Henrietta could not catch them. She was not fast but she was strong—much stronger than they were.

A few years later, Henry and Henrietta's older brother Peter returned home to the farm after his tour in the European conflict. He had received severe burns when the tank he had been in was hit by enemy fire. His hands were still very tender and sensitive from the burns. He wanted to work on the farm, but his hands had to be protected. His job was to operate the tractor and binder with his brother Henry.

The backbreaking task of setting up the stooks fell upon their sisters. As the two brothers were operating the machinery, Peter commented to Henry that Henrietta's stooks looked as strong as a prairie outhouse. Henry paused, and with a twinkle in his steel blue eyes, said to his brother, "Watch how we can make Henrietta as mad as a mother cluck." Henry and his brother drove the tractor past a stook Henrietta had just set up. Henry slowed the tractor down to snail speed and whispered to his brother just loud enough so that Henrietta could hear, "*Shhh, sie stell, moak den Kjätel stell, ooda woat Yet äare Goawe äwa faule* (Shhh, be quiet, throttle the engine or Henrietta's stooks will topple over)!" Henry got the desired result. He slammed the tractor into high gear before the bolting Henrietta could get close to him and Peter.

Eva's Stooks

Peter S. and Katharina Hildebrand
|
Katharina Maria Olga Helen Anna Peter Abram **Henrietta Henry Eva**

Stooking. Just hearing the word "stooking" made Eva shudder. She couldn't think of a single nice word to say about stooking. Picking up those itchy bundles of sheaves was hard, back-breaking work. The rickety old binder had supposedly tied the sheaves. Its job was to tie sheaves so that they could easily be set up into little straw tent-like structures. The purpose of these stook tents was to expose the grain that was delicately attached to the stocks to the warm summer sun. The sun gently sucked all the moisture out of each separate grain. Once all the grain was dry, the stooks were hoisted into the hungry threshing machine to separate the grain from the chaff.

The process of stooking was very hard work, but no kid raised on a southern Manitoba farm in the '30s was exempt from the task. The term "conscientious objector" was not a part of the vocabulary until 1939 when Mennonite sons were conscripted into the military.

If "conscientious objector" had been a part of the daily vocabulary, many kids would have used the words to get exempted from stooking. They would have based their argument on the grounds that they did not want to do battle with the sheaves and that stooking brought out the evil in them. It caused their language to be less than fitting, their tempers to rise above boiling point on the old Fahrenheit thermometer, and their behaviours to be truly unchristian. Therefore, they should not have to stook.

Eva did her best to escape from the task of stooking. She tapped into the creative side of her brain to figure out how she could avoid dealing with that scratchy crop of oats, amid swarms of Manitoba mosquitoes that were ravenous for the blood of a fine little Mennonite girl.

Hard as she tried to get out of it, she had to go to the nearby Edenthal farm, to stook with her

Sketch by Katie Altendorf Cable © 2003

– Story told to the author by her Aunt Eva on the way to *Taunte Trütji's* funeral. Eva's sister Henrietta was there to hear the story and add snippets to it.

brother Henry and her sister Henrietta. Henry and Henrietta were busy stooking, and Eva went through the motions, pretending to be as busy as they were. Slowly she worked her way in a direction away from her siblings. Once she was as far away from them as possible, she built herself a fine sturdy stook that could not be blown over by gale winds or fall apart in torrential rains. It was truly an architect's delight.

Eva positioned the bundles into a perfect teepee, just big enough for her tiny body to enter. There she sat like a rolled-up mouse, away from the blistering sun, the pesky mosquitoes, and from her brother and sister. It didn't take long before they were calling her, "*Efji, Efji, wua best dü* (Eva, Eva, where are you)?" Eva's lips were glued shut. She only got smaller and quieter in her tent. Henry and Henrietta didn't spend much time calling her because they had a lot of work to do before their father came to conduct a quality control check on their work.

They struggled and strained to get their work done by inspection time. Finally, all the work was done and their father came to check their work. Only then did little Eva emerge from her personally crafted harbor. She greeted her brother and sister with a big Cheshire smile. They did not respond in kind. They did not say what they wanted to say to their sister Eva. She was the baby and they knew that the sun rose and set on little Eva.

Henry's First Crop

Peter S. and Katharina Hildebrand | Johan M. and Helena Sawatzky
| |
Henry | Anna

Nineteen-forty-seven, the year Henry Hildebrand married pretty Anna Sawatzky from Blumenthal, was the first year Henry earned wages by farming. For years Henry had worked on the farm that his father Peter had bought from his father. Peter had never considered paying his son a wage. After all, Henry had room and board at home and, in Peter's opinion, he had enough spending money. Peter understood that things were different now that his son had a young wife. His son would need an income and more independence or Peter could not be sure that Henry and his Anna would stay on the farm.

Peter paid Henry by letting him have the earnings from eighteen acres of land. The remaining quarter section of the Edenburg farm remained in Peter's control.

Henry seeded fifteen acres of flax and three acres of wheat that first year of farming the eighteen acres. The land produced an outstanding crop. The flax field yielded twenty bushels to the acre and the price for flax was $5.50 per bushel that year.

Henry's cousin Ed hauled the shiny brown flaxseed to C.V.O. (Co-Op Vegetable Oils) in his three-ton truck. He returned with a cheque of $1,000.00 in his hands. It was the largest cheque that C.V.O. had ever issued for one truckload of grain and it was Henry's wage for the year.

– Told to the author by her father, Henry D. Hildebrand in June, 2001

Horse Medicine

Johan M. and Helena Sawatzky
|
Tina Nettie Heinrich **Jakob** Mary Helen Marge Anna John Diedrich Willie

Early one morning when Jakob was feeding the barn animals, he realized something was wrong with one of the horses that was used for the farm field work. The horse could not get up on its four legs. It tried and tried again to stand, but it stumbled, only to remain lying listless on the barn floor. Jakob rushed indoors to tell his father about the horse's odd behaviour. Surely his father Johan would know what to do. After all, Jakob's father's was Johan M. Sawatzky and Johan M. was well recognized for his veterinary skills. No one knew where or how he learned them, but everyone knew he had talent.

Johan dropped everything and raced to the barn to inspect the sickly horse. No farmer could afford to lose a good hard-working horse. He examined the horse very closely, felt the horse's body here and there, watched the horse's futile attempts to stand up, and then made a decision about what to do.

Johan ordered Jakob to get two ten-foot long belts from the threshing machine. Jakob obediently fetched the two belts even though he didn't have a clue about his father's intentions. Johan gently slung one belt all around the horse directly behind its front legs, and he slung the second belt around the horse directly in front of the hind legs. He attached both belts to the hay lift at the end of the barn. Under normal circumstances, the hay lift was used to lift hay into the hayloft from the ground floor, but this time it was used to lift a horse. Once the belts were securely attached to the hay lift, the hay lift was raised, pulling the horse up to a standing position, and then just a little higher. The horse's hooves could barely touch the ground so that the horse did not bear weight on its limbs.

Johan had not yet finished the medical procedure. He could tell that the horse had an infection. He made two incisions on each side of the horse's chest with a *Flett*, a sharp cutting tool designed to make surgical incisions in livestock. Then he laced a string from one incision to the next as though they were eyelets in a shoe. The incisions allowed the infection to drain from the horse, and young Jakob

– Story told by Jakob Sawatzky at the July 14, 2001 Sawatzky reunion.

watched as the pus oozed out of the incisions.

The horse was suspended from the hay lift for a week. Jakob brought feed and water to the horse every day. With encouraging words and a gentle neck rub, Jakob urged the horse to get better. One morning Jakob went to the barn as usual, and was amazed and delighted to see the horse beginning to stand on all four hooves. Jakob dropped his pail full of feed, and ran inside to tell his father, "*Daut Peat es meist bäta* (The horse is almost better)." And so it was.

For years, a photograph of the horse, working with a threshing gang, hung on Jakob's workshop wall. The picture was taken after the horse regained good health. It was a testimonial to Johan's divine veterinarian intervention and to Jakob's affection for the four-legged beast. It cannot be denied that Jakob's love helped the horse get better.

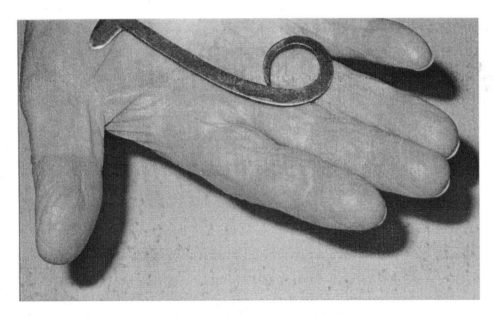

Bloodletting instrument used for large animals by Johan Sawatzky
(courtesy of Jakob Sawatzky)

Johan – The Veterinarian Ophthalmologist

Johan M. and Helena Sawatzky

|

Tina Nettie Heinrich Jakob Mary Helen Marge Anna John Diedrich Willie

Johan would not even think of paying a veterinarian good money to save the life of one of his cows or horses. Johan took care of his own animals' medical concerns—including their eye problems.

Occasionally one of his cows got an oat kernel in her eye. The entire eye turned white like a cataract. It looked like a tiny sheet of white flannel was tucked under the cow's eyelid. For the cow, that meant she could not see, and that she was very uncomfortable. How could she find the juiciest stems of grass in the pasture if she could not see them? How could she know where to find her stall in the barn for milking time if she had no vision? Johan knew how to make things better for the cow. He looked for a smooth, clean stick. If he could not find a smooth, clean stick, he cut a twig from a tree, and slowly whittled it to a velvety finish with the pocket knife he always carried in his pocket. The next step was less pleasant. Using the smooth, clean stick, Johan scraped up human deposits from the toilet, or from a baby's soiled diaper. He gently applied the excrement to the animal's eye with the stick like salve to a wound. The eye cleared up. The little white flannel sheet that coated the cow's eye disappeared.

It causes one to wonder where the term "Here's mud in your eye" came from. After all, polite company probably would not say, "Here's poop in your eye!"

– Story told to the author by her Uncle Jakob J. Sawatzky, October 31, 2001.

"Lunch Break" by Mary Elias © 1997 by Pembina Threshermans Museum

Health and Wellness

Typically only people with extra cash visited the dentist or the doctor. Usually the reason to visit a dentist was to remove any stubborn remaining teeth and to be fitted for dentures. It was not uncommon for Mennonite youths to get their first set of dentures around their 16th year. Filling teeth was virtually unheard of, and baby teeth were never filled. It hurt to have teeth drilled and filled, and it was much cheaper to get a mouthful of artificial teeth.

Self-made healers were often sought out before visiting a college-trained doctor. The service of the self-made healers was provided for a small fee or a donation. There were private practices throughout southern Manitoba. *Trachtmoaka* (right maker, or chiropractor, often called a knibbler) Hildebrand from the village of Sommerfeld had patients visit him from miles away. He had a good reputation for making people "better". *Trachtmoaka* Hildebrand used *Apodoldok* to massage every strain or pain that crossed the threshold of his house. He recommended that his patients buy the clear glass bottles filled with the transparent alcohol-based yellowish-brown liquid from him. He used so much *Apodoldok* that his "waiting room" reeked of the potent medication.

Alcohol based remedies were common. Johan M. Sawatzky prescribed apricot brandy and sugar to cure the common cold. His wife Helena's favourite medication for her stomach ailments was 40 percent proof *Alpenkräuter* (herbs from the Alps in liquid form). *Alpenkräuter* soothed her *Moag* (stomach) and its side effects calmed her nerves.

Bloodletting

Johan M. and **Helena** Sawatzky
|
Tina Nettie Heinrich Jakob Helen Mary Marge Anna John Diedrich Willie

Johan M. Sawatzky practiced the medical art, or perhaps the medical science, of blood letting. It was believed that bloodletting, the practice of letting "patients" bleed, reduced their blood pressure. Folks who were not even Mennonite went to see Johan for bloodletting treatments.

Johan's surgical equipment for the procedure consisted of a *Baunt* (string) which was used as a tourniquet and a special bloodletting tool called a *Flett*, which ejected a blade into the patient's veins like a stiletto. The patient's blood dripped into a large enamel bowl from Johan's wife Helena's kitchen.

Helena was Johan's "surgical assistant". She prepared the equipment Johan needed and washed it up after the surgery. Her daughters had the unpleasant and dreaded job of dispensing with the blood after the bloodletting was done.

On the patient's first visit, Johan made a few cursory inquiries regarding the patient's medical condition. Then he carefully and firmly tied the *Baunt* around the patient's upper arm, and pierced the vein with the stiletto-like tool. Blood flowed freely from the incision into the flowered enamel bowl.

Once enough blood had been drawn, according to Johan's program, he pierced a straight pin through the skin on each side of the bleeding cut, making an X with the cut and the straight pin. Johan plucked a single hair from his patient's head and wrapped the hair around the pin like an infinity sign, or like an 8 lying on its side. The patient was free to go home. Johan did not recommend follow up visits. His assumption was that if people did not come back on their own accord, they were well.

Johan received patients from far and wide. If the people who drove on to the yard were not Mennonites, then it was certain that they had come for a "medical procedure". One day when some Emerson folks came by for a bloodletting treatment Johan's assistant Helena was not home.

Johan assumed his daughter Nettie would simply take over the job that was typically his wife's job. There was no orientation. Johan directed Nettie, "*Netji, hol mie den Baunt* (Nettie, get me the string)." Nettie wanted no part of this bloodletting business. Just to think about participating in the process made her heart race and skip beats. She was so upset to think about helping her father with his "surgery", that she had to lie down to calm

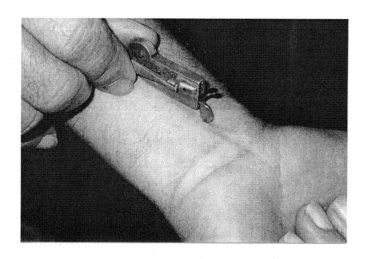

Bloodletting instrument used by Johan Sawatzky
(courtesy of Bill Neufeld)

herself. She knew someone had to do the job, but it was not going to be her. Innocent as pie, she said to her sister Tina, "*Tien nü motts du Papi den Baunt hole gone. Ekj sie fäl tow schwack* (Tina, now you must get father the string. I am much too weak)." Tina was older than Nettie, but she was the meek and mild daughter. She did her sister's bidding, but she hated the job as much as Nettie did.

Each of Johan's daughters had a turn at the odious job of discarding patients' blood. They all despised it and tried to be out of sight when it came time for the job to be done. Eventually Tina and Nettie mustered up their courage to tell their mother "*Wan Papi daut doone well, dan kaun hee daut Bloot blooss selfst opp rieme* (If father wants to do that, then he can clean the blood up himself)." Helena may have shared her daughters' aversion to the blood disposal job with her husband, and then again, she may not have. In any case, Johan finally did give up his "practice" and no one was happier than his daughters.

Dora Learns About Bloodletting

Johan M. and **Helena** Sawatzky

|

Tina Nettie Heinrich Jakob Mary Helen Marge Anna John Diedrich Willie

|

Dora

Often when nine-year-old Dora visited her grandma and grandpa in Blumenthal, she saw strangers coming to see her grandpa, Johan Sawatzky, at the house. Dora's grandma, Helena, ushered the guests into the living room where Johan greeted them. Helena left the room and closed the door behind her. This in itself was somewhat suspicious to Dora because that living room door was always open.

Dora's questions about what was going on behind the closed door were met with her grandma's "*Kjinja Froage met Tsocka bestreit* (Children's questions sprinkled with sugar)," which really meant "don't ask; I won't tell you." Dora was not allowed to enter that room until her grandpa's guests said their good byes.

One day a certain man came to visit her grandpa. Johan and the gentleman visitor went into the living room, closing the door behind them. They spoke in hushed tones behind the closed door. Usually, no one, not even Helena, was allowed in the room until after the visitor left. This time was different. Dora's grandpa and the visitor seemed to be in the room for a very long time when suddenly a loud voice was heard from the living room. It was Johan. His voice sounded urgent and frightened. Johan called Helena into the room. She recognized the urgency in his voice and hurried into the living room, quickly closing the door behind her.

Soon she returned. Her face was ashen. Helena was holding a blue galvanized bowl filled with blood, which was thickening like Jell-O. She handed the bowl with its jelling contents to the young Dora, and firmly instructed her to dump the contents in the thistle patch behind the wooden red chicken barn. Dora saw from her grandma's grim face that this was not the time to question or to argue with her. She carried the bowl out carefully so as not to spill any of the red liquid on to herself or on to the floor. She did not understand any of this, but it made her heart beat like the drum she had heard in the Rhineland Agricultural Society parade.

When Dora returned to the house with the stained bowl, Johan's guest was leaving. Before the guest was off the farmyard, Dora started asking questions. "*Groospapi*, where did that blood come from?" "*Groosmama*, how did that blood get into that bowl?" "What were you doing in that room, *Groospapi*?"

Johan and Helena had to answer their granddaughter's questions. They could not leave her without answers now that she had seen all that blood.

Dora learned about how her grandpa helped people with high blood pressure. She learned that people came to her grandpa for bloodletting in order to lower their blood pressure. This one time it seemed that too much blood had been let, and the "patient" was experiencing complications. Dora's grandpa had not known what to do except to call his wife.

That was the very last time Johan treated people for their high blood pressure. Johan believed he could help people. This time he was afraid that he might have harmed someone. He never wanted that to happen. Johan was very frightened.

Waulle Lein's Toothache

John M. and Helena Sawatzky
|
Tina Heinrich **Nettie** Jakob Helen Mary Marge Anna John Diedrich Willie

---

Nettie's friend *Waulle Lein* (Wall's Helen) had an excruciating toothache. In her mind, having the tooth pulled would be so much less painful than her toothache. *Waulle Lein* figured that comparing the two pains was like comparing a mosquito bite to an amputation. *Waulle Lein* was one tough cookie!

Her friend Nettie's father pulled teeth and he did not charge any money. *Waulle Lein* asked Nettie's father Johan if he might give consideration to pulling her tooth. She showed him which tooth she wanted to have extracted. She opened her mouth wide, and with her stubby finger, softly touched the tooth that was giving her so much misery.

Johan unlocked his writing desk where he kept his tooth pulling tongs. Before he could get near to her mouth with the tongs, she looked deep into Johan's dark brown eyes and asked, "*Oomkji Sawatsji, ha jie Narfe* (Mr. Sawatzky, do you have nerve)?" What she really meant, was "Do you have the guts to pull my tooth, old man?"

Johan did not miss a beat. He answered the brash *Waulle Lein* with a curt "*Jo*". He grasped his tooth pulling tongs, gripped the tooth, and pulled…and pulled…and pulled. The tooth would not budge. Johan called his two eldest sons, Heinrich and Jakob, to hold *Waulle Lein* down because Johan's firm grip on the tooth was pulling the girl off of her stool. Johan showed *Waulle Lein* that he had nerve. He pulled and pulled until the tooth came out. Throughout the entire ordeal, *Waulle Lein* did not make a peep. She was going to show that Johan M. Sawatzky that she too had "*Narfe*" of steel.

– Story told to the author by her aunts Nettie Neufeld and Mary Hildebrand May 31, 2001.

Henrietta's Toothache

Peter S. and Katharina Hildebrand   Heinrich Hildebrand

Henrietta

Henrietta had secretly cried all night. She was in the worst pain she had ever experienced in her few short years. Even though her pain was excruciating, Henrietta was determined that no one would see tears leak from her eyes. It would be beneath her dignity to let anyone know that she was crying. Crying was for babies and Henrietta was already thirteen. She tried to make pictures of nice things in her head, but her toothache let her think of nothing else but the pain. She fought back the tears that were welling up behind her eyelids.

She knew that people often went to see her Uncle Henry Hildebrand to have their teeth pulled. Her Uncle Henry did just that—he pulled teeth with a pair of tongs. He used no anaesthetic to hide the pain. He did not fill teeth with gold or silver. He had never heard of a root canal. He pulled teeth.

Henrietta walked east along the dusty dirt road to her Uncle Henry's house. Little clouds of dust rose around her ankles as she dragged one foot after the other. As she walked, her hand cupped her painful and swollen mouth. She had decided to ask her uncle if he would pull her tooth for her. She could think of no other alternative to take away the ache. Her Uncle Henry was a kind and a gentle man. He asked Henrietta to open her mouth wide. She opened it as wide as she could, and he looked inside. He could not help but notice the tear-stained face that she had been trying so hard to hide. He felt sorry for his brother's daughter. He knew how painful toothaches could be, but he also knew how much it hurt to have a tooth pulled. He did not want to inflict any more pain on his niece than she had already endured, but there was no choice. The tooth, that was to have been permanent, had to come out. Henrietta's uncle got out his tongs from the case where he stored them and, as gently as possible, he pulled the rotten tooth.

Henrietta endured the extraction without a sob. Her Uncle Henry checked inside her mouth and announced to her, *"De Tän biesied disse es uck gauns*

– Story told to the author by her Aunt Henrietta Schroeder on March 25, 2002.

fefült (The tooth beside this one is also completely rotten)."

Quietly, but without a moment's hesitation, Henrietta responded, "*Dout dee uck üt riete* (Pull that one out too)."

Her uncle could barely believe his ears. Hadn't he inflicted enough pain on her already?

The young girl sat, as brave as a young soldier who had not experienced war, as she waited for her uncle to pull the second decayed tooth. Again, he pulled the tooth as gently as he could, but it broke in two. He had to pull out the remaining piece of the tooth, and Henrietta would have to withstand pain as though she was having three teeth pulled. Henrietta held her ground. Her body tensed into one big muscle and her hands got slippery wet, but she neither cried nor whimpered.

Much later, her uncle boasted that he had never seen a young girl as brave as his niece Henrietta. His niece mused that her Uncle Henry had no idea how much worse the toothache was than the actual extractions.

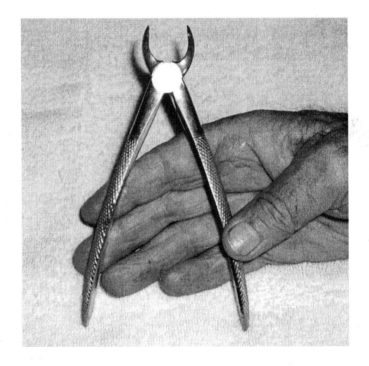

Tongs used by Henrietta's uncle, Henry Hildebrand
(courtesy of Anna Hildebrand)

Johan the Dentist

Johan M. Sawatzky and Helena Sawatzky

|

Tina Nettie Heinrich Jakob Helen Mary Marge Anna John Diedrich Willie

---

Johan's varnished oak desk beside his rocking chair was angled against the corner of the smoky living room. His silver coloured metal spittoon sat on the polished linoleum floor beside the rocking chair. His wife Helena's fuchsia-coloured impatiens and red geraniums planted in cans labeled Roger's Golden Syrup were perched on the high glossy-white windowsills. The flowers did their best to cheer up the room.

Johan's favourite seat in the house was his rocking chair. It was as if he was guarding the contents of his desk. None of his grandchildren ever dared go into that writing desk. They all knew what was inside it. Besides the usual pencils, ink well and papers of interest only to their grandpa and the government, the desk also contained a metal box. All the children knew what was inside the box, and they never wanted their grandpa to open it. That box only came out on rare occasions and the grandchildren dreaded those times.

When the children drove to their grandma and grandpa's house with their moms and dads, they knew whether that box would come out of the writing desk. The box held pliers especially designed to pull teeth and if any of the children had a toothache or a loose tooth stubbornly hanging to the gums, their grandpa pulled out the pliers and removed the aching or loose teeth. The metal box only ever came out for the kids—never for the adults.

Johan invited the little ones to his chair where he was sitting. The fearful children had to tell their grandpa which tooth was hurting or loose. Often they had to repeat themselves several times because their grandpa's hearing aid didn't always pick up the tones of quiet children—especially scared, quiet children.

They watched as Johan took out the cold silver pliers, that looked an awful lot like the pliers their daddies used for fixing machinery. Johan grasped the tooth with his tooth pulling pliers and pulled. He used no anaesthetic or sterilizers, and Johan never got paid for his services.

After an extraction, their Grandma Helena gave the children a glass of warm salt water to rinse out their mouths. Then came the real treat that each child looked forward to after having a tooth pulled.

They got to spit into their grandpa's spittoon—their one and only opportunity. The best part was if their grandma gave them lots of warm salt water. That meant that they could spit really hard and *spritz* the water into the spittoon like a fireman's water hose.

Crime and Punishment

He who spares the rod hates his son, but he who loves him is diligent to discipline him.
Proverbs 13:24

Society in general accepted that corporal punishment was an appropriate method of teaching children how to behave. The community and the church were supportive of spanking, although they did not approve of beating children. It was not always clear where one started and the other ended.

Spare the Rod

Peter S. and Katharina Hildebrand
|
Katharina Maria Olga **Helen** Anna **Peter** Abram Henrietta Henry Eva

Peter S. Hildebrand believed in God and in the Bible. He paid particular attention to the verse that addressed the issue of raising children, "Spare the rod and spoil the child". He embraced the same interpretation as did all the other fathers of his time. If parents did not use the rod, then surely their children would be spoiled. Peter S. knew what that meant—if he did not use a rod to punish his children, then his children would grow up to be irresponsible, unchristian citizens. It was generally understood that the rod was intended to spank children. It was not understood that the rod was intended to guide children, as a shepherd would use a rod to guide his sheep.

Peter S. did not see the need to spank his children every time they committed a transgression. Instead, he chose to keep a weekly count of each one of his children's wrong doings. Then, on Saturdays, he reminded his children, item by item, of every wrong that they had committed during the week. After reciting the list of transgressions, he spanked each child according to how bad and how frequent their sins had been during the week.

Peter's first born son, Peter, along with his brothers and sisters, had to stand before his father to listen to the list of his weekly sins before his father applied the rod to his backside. It did not take young Peter

– On May 1999, this story was told to the author by her aunt, Anne Schellenberg and her uncle, Peter Hildebrand.

long to learn that when his father spanked him, the length of the spanking depended upon how loud and how quickly he wailed. Young Peter started to wail even before the spanking started so that it would come to a speedy ending.

Young Peter's older sister Helen did not subscribe to that strategy. Helen was a particularly headstrong young girl, and she was not about to protest loudly. When it was her turn to listen to her errors of omissions and commissions, and receive her due punishment, she refused to cry when the rod was applied to her rear. It was a battle of will between father and daughter. What would last longer—the father's spanking or the daughter's refusal to cry?

The senior Peter thought that Helen had to cry because crying was a sign of remorse.

After one of their father and daughter confrontations, the senior Peter confided to his wife Katharina, "*Daut jinkj mie nijch scheen* (I did not enjoy that)." That did not mean that he usually enjoyed spanking his children. It was his way of saying how badly he felt about having to spank Helen so hard and so long in order to teach her remorse. His children were supposed to feel remorse for their transgressions. If his Helen did not cry, that meant that she had not learned her lesson, and that was not right. What could he do about her?

Spoil the Child

Johan M. and **Helena** Sawatzky
|
Tina **Nettie** Heinrich Jakob Helena Maria Marge Anna John Diedrich Willie

Johan and his wife Helena believed that the Bible quotation to spare the rod and spoil the child meant that if they did not use the rod enough, their children would be spoiled. That was interpreted to mean that if children did not get spanked enough with a rod or a strap or a stick, they would not grow up to be responsible, God-fearing adults. Helena and Johan were determined that their children would not be spoiled. Their children would all become good citizens in the community and in the church. At the time when they were raising their children, it was acceptable and expected that parents used physical punishment when their children's behaviours needed correcting. Not to spank their children was frowned upon by the community. Not to spank meant that parents were shirking their responsibilities as parents. Everyone spanked their children. Everyone wanted to raise their children right.

Helena and Johan's second daughter Nettie was almost always a hard-working, obedient girl. She dried the dishes when her mother told her to. She milked the fat, cud-chewing cows lined up in a row in the barn when her father reminded her. Nettie also refrained from doing things that she had been taught were wrong. That meant that she would never, ever, talk back to her father.

Nettie was a well-behaved child, but she was also a willful young lass and she had her own unique way of making her personal opinions known. One day her parents were planning to visit her aunt's home and Nettie fully expected to join them because her aunt had two daughters, Mary and Helen. Nettie loved to play with them. Nettie was already looking forward to the fun that she, Helen, and Mary would have. They would play with dolls and play hide-and-seek while their parents would sit on chairs like old people and just talk.

Nettie's parents had other plans, and they did not include Nettie. She had to stay home with the maid* and her brothers and sisters. Staying at home with the maid and her brothers and sisters would be so boring. Nettie was very disappointed,

– Story told to the author by her Aunt Nettie Neufeld during a visit with Nettie in her Altona condominium on January 11, 2002.

* It was common practice to have a local girl live with a family to help with domestic duties. When Johan and Helena's daughters were old enough, they also worked as maids for neighbours and relatives. Often the parents made the employment arrangements on behalf of the girls.

but she did not dare argue with her parents. Oh no, that would never do. Nettie had another way of showing her disappointment and anger.

While the parents were away, the maid baked a cake. When she pulled the perfectly done cake from the clay bake oven, its aroma wafted in the air to tempt the hungry children. Nettie approached the cake as if to admire it, and as fast as the maid could say "*Oba Mejal* (Oh but, girl)," Nettie poked her finger into the cake, spoiling its lovely smooth finish, and flattening it. The maid gasped with shock. This little angelic hard-working girl had just committed such a mean-spirited act, that the maid had no choice. She would have to report the incident to Nettie's parents.

True to her word, no sooner had Johan M. and Helena returned home from their visit, when the maid reported the cake-poking incident in great detail. Cake-poking was not tolerated in the Sawatzky household. Nettie knew it and her parents knew it. Johan invited Nettie into the

room where he administered punishment to the backside of his children. Once in that room, he proceeded to give Nettie a spanking she would never forget.

After each whack on the bottom with a leather strap, he asked his daughter, "*Woascht dü daut wada doone* (Will you do that again)?" Nettie understood him to say, "*Woascht dü daut nijch wada doone* (Will you not do that again)?" and replied "*Jo*," repeatedly, thinking she was agreeing that she would never do that again.

After each *Jo*, Nettie received another whack on her bottom. Her father had never seen his little girl be quite so willful. He could not understand why she would poke a cake again even when she knew she should not do that. He finally gave up and decided that his Nettie had been punished enough for a little finger poke in the cake.

Kerosene Lamp Fiasco

Johan M. and Helena Sawatzky
|
Tina **Nettie** Heinrich Jakob Helena Mary Marge Anna John Diedrich Willie

Nettie was pleased as cherry pie that her aunt and uncle had come to visit and that their daughter Mary had come along with them. Mary was Nettie's cousin and her extra good friend. Nettie knew for sure that she and Mary would have lots of fun. They would giggle, tell each other secrets, and play games.

It was late in the day and getting dark when Mary and her parents arrived. Nettie's mother reminded Nettie, "*Neetji, daut es meist diesta, go hole mol de Laump fonn de Benkj aune Waunt* (Nettie, it is almost dark, go get the lamp from the shelf on the wall)." Nettie quickly went to get a clear glass kerosene lamp with the black trimmed wick from the shelf in the pantry that smelled like sour milk. She was eager to do what her mother told her to do, because the sooner she got the job done, the sooner she and Mary could play.

Nettie was a small girl and she had to step on her tippy toes to reach the row of kerosene lamps lined up on the wooden shelf. She stretched as far as she could to reach the kerosene filled glass lamp closest to her. She had just touched the lamp with the tip of her longest finger, when the entire shelf crashed to the floor, glass lamps and all. It sounded like a bomb exploding in the deepest part of the night. There were sharp shards of broken glass and splashed kerosene all over the floor and walls.

Nettie was mortified. She could not believe what had just happened. All she could think of was how angry her mother would be with her. Nettie forgot all about playing with her cousin. She just wanted to get out of that room. Punishment was surely on the doorstep for Nettie. She raced out of the pantry that now smelled of kerosene instead of sour milk. She ran up the brown painted wooden stairs and into her bed. She wept scalding tears of shame and embarrassment. She felt sick. Her heart was as heavy as the giant stone in the pasture. Nettie cried until her eyes were red and swollen. She never did play with her cousin Mary that evening. She was so scared and she felt so horrible about what she had done. She knew that

– Told to the author by her Aunt Nettie Neufeld on January 12, 2002.

Sketch by Katie Altendorf Cable © 2003

she was big enough to get the lamps from the shelf in the pantry that smelled like sour milk. She had done it lots of times. She shouldn't have let the lamps fall—and they would cost a lot of money to replace.

The next morning she went down the stairs, quiet as a shadow, wishing she was invisible. Nettie was fearful of the punishment that was most certainly waiting for her. No one said a word about the broken lamps and the spilled kerosene. No one said "*Neetji, daut wea nijch diene Schult* (Nettie that wasn't your fault)," to comfort her.

The stone stayed on her heart and no one lifted if for her to make her feel better. Not saying anything was her parents' only way of saying, "Accidents happen, and it's not your fault." Nettie would have loved to hear those words to make her feel better, but that was just not the way things were done.

When Mama and Papa Were Out

Johan M. and Helena Sawatzky

|

Tina Nettie **Heinrich** Jakob Helena Mary Marge Anna John Diedrich Willie

Heinrich was Johan and Helena's first-born son. In his mind, that gave him special liberties that the other children in the family did not have.

For the most part, when his parents were home, Heinrich behaved as well as his younger brothers and sisters did, even though he often added an attitude of arrogance and wrath to his menu of behaviours. That was just to remind his brothers and sisters that he was the oldest boy in the family and ought to be treated with due respect. When Helena and Johan left home and Heinrich knew they would be away for some time, his behaviour took a dramatic turn. The dust raised by his parents' car as they drove off the yard down the dirt lane had not settled before Heinrich made a beeline to the soft velvety sofa in the living room. There he lay down as comfortably as a house cat. His feet dangled over one end of the sofa, and at the other end, his muscled arms propped up his head.

No sooner was Heinrich in this regal relaxed position, than he started to give orders to his siblings as though he was a king and they were his royal, but not necessarily loyal, subjects. "*Hauns hol mi waut Knacksot* (Johnny get me some sunflower seeds)"; "*Diedrich, sie stell* (Diedrich, be quiet)"; or "*Marieche, go moak mie Koffe* (Mary, go make me coffee)." If his little subjects did not follow his directions, Heinrich wasted no time in taking matters into his own hands. For the little ruffians who dared to defy him, he served a speedy tongue-lashing or a little cuff to show them who was boss while his Mama and Papa were away.

It did not take long before Heinrich rose from his restful perch, sauntered over to his father's writing desk, and unlocked it. His father never left the key for the children to find. The children, including Heinrich, had no business in his writing desk where he stored his dentistry tools, his account

– Story told to the author by her Uncle Dick (Diedrich Sawatzky) during a visit to his home in British Columbia on May 9, 2002

books, a bottle of apricot brandy to treat colds, and his stash of finely cut tobacco.

Heinrich had no need for his father's key. His father had taught his eldest son to be a resourceful and creative young man. This paid off for Heinrich. He wasted no time using those skills to his best advantage. He fashioned himself a key from a square nail intended to shoe horses. The key fit perfectly into the writing desk keyhole. Heinrich opened up the desk, reached for the tobacco tin, and helped himself to a generous plug of tobacco and some very thin rectangular Zig Zag cigarette papers to roll himself a smoke or two. He locked up the desk, making sure everything was as he had found it, so as not to raise his father's suspicions. He knew only too well what the punishment for theft would be if his father found out.

Heinrich sat back down on the sofa. He expertly rolled himself a cigarette as he had seen his father do many times. Heinrich had developed his own expertise from the many times that he had broken into his father's writing desk. Before he had finished rolling his cigarette, he ordered his young brothers "*Diedrich ouda Willie, go hol mie mol ni Schwäwel* (Diedrich or Willie, go get me a match)." The boys scrambled to do their brother's bidding.

The little children could not wait for their parents to return home, but they never tattled. It was curious that Heinrich's father never noticed the missing tobacco, nor did he notice that the keyhole was getting larger. Or did he?

Papa Can I Go Out?

Johan M. and Helena Sawatzky
|
Tina **Nettie** Heinrich Jakob Helen Mary Marge Anna John Diedrich Willie

If the Sawatzky girls wanted to go out with their friends, the rule was that they had to ask their parents' permission before they went out. The rule was set in cement.

The problem was that very often their parents Johan and Helena Sawatzky went visiting for the whole day and the evening, leaving their teenagers at home. That meant that if friends came to the house to invite one of the girls out, the girl had no way of getting her parents' permission. There was no way to communicate with the parents. The rule about asking permission to go out applied even if the parents were not at home. It was unthinkable to telephone the parents. Telephone calls were for important matters and social matters were not considered important enough to telephone about—especially not a teenager's social life. Even the adults never telephoned ahead when they went to visit someone. They just dropped in on friends or neighbours unannounced and were made welcome.

One fine summer Sunday evening when her parents were out visiting, friends came to call on Nettie, and asked her to go out with them. Nettie desperately wanted to join her friends. An evening with her friends promised to be plenty of fun.

Nettie was torn. She knew that if she went with her friends without parental permission, there would be a high price to pay. She knew the rule, but she was oh, so tempted to break it. What should she do?

She took the risk. She chose to go out with her friends without permission. Her choice was to have fun and to pay the price later. And pay she did. When she got home from her evening of fun with her friends, her father was waiting for her. How dare she break the rules? Johan was bristling with anger. He had a lecture for Nettie that she would never forget. Nettie heard all about the dangers of young girls not listening to their parents, and about how her reputation in the community would be besmirched with her reckless behaviour.

– This story was told to the author by her Aunt Nettie Neufeld, when they visited on January 11, 2002.

Above all, he wondered whether his young Nettie had given any thought to what people would think of him if he could not get his daughter to obey her own father.

Nettie saw the injustice of this. How could she ask permission when her parents were not home? They knew very well that when the young people went out, their plans only came together at the eleventh hour. It was not as though Nettie could predict that her friends would come calling. If she had asked her parents early in the day whether she could go out in the event that friends might invite her, she could be considered vain or proud. How could she think that she was so popular that friends would come calling on her? That would never do for a young Mennonite girl who had been taught to be humble.

Nettie took it upon herself to address this issue with her mother. She would never dare address this concern with her father. That would have taken more courage than Nettie could dig up.

Nettie reminded her mother that when young people came calling, they did not plan ahead. That was the way things were done. She also reminded her mother that by the time the young people came calling, her mother and father were usually already out visiting, and she couldn't ask their permission. That meant that Nettie had to miss out on heaps of fun with her friends. Her mother fully understood her daughter's dilemma. She simply sighed with a "*Na jo, soo es ji daut dann* (well yes, that is the way it is)."

Nettie's discussion with her mother did not change the way her parents did business. Nevertheless, Nettie made herself a promise. She told herself that if she ever had children, they would not have to ask for her permission each time they wanted to go out with their friends. Nettie kept that promise.

Learning Social Graces

Johan M. and Helena Sawatzky
|
Tina Nettie Heinrich **Jakob** Helen Mary Marge Anna John **Diedrich** Willie

Certain subjects of conversation were absolutely taboo. There were some things that children should not know about. If they accidentally heard a conversation regarding certain delicate subjects, they should know enough to pretend that they were not hearing what was being said. One such delicate subject was the topic of pregnancy. Children were never informed when a new baby was expected in the family. When a new baby did arrive, it came as a complete surprise to all the youngsters in the family.

Even women did not speak openly of pregnancies amongst themselves. When they referred to pregnancy, they discussed it very privately and spoke in euphemisms such as "*de es aulwada so*" (she is like that again) or "*de es enne Bloom*" (she is in flower).

Nine-year old Diedrich had noticed that his older brother Jakob's young wife was getting quite big around her middle. This came as a surprise to Diedrich because he remembered that at their wedding, Helen had been a tall, striking, and slim bride. With a twinkle in his eye, and just a little smirk, Diedrich felt compelled to make his observation known to Jakob, saying, "*Daut wud so lote daut diene Lena aul en groota Buck haft* (It would look as though your Helen already has a big stomach)." Jakob could not believe the nerve of his brother. He was such a cheeky little brat! Jakob was upset and he was embarrassed by the suggestion from his little brother. Jakob knew that it was not his job to discipline his brother, but he felt it was his duty to inform their father of how brash young Diedrich had been. Perhaps his father would help Diedrich understand about the etiquette of how not to speak about newly married women who quickly got thick around the middle. Diedrich should know never to mention such things. Such things were private and secret.

Their father agreed that Diedrich needed to be taught manners. Diedrich could not go about making such grave social errors. To make comments about a woman's girth when she was probably with child was to acknowledge a pregnancy, and Diedrich was far too young to even think about such things—they thought. He had been told that storks delivered babies, and that is what he should believe. Now, if Diedrich would have commented on someone who was simply becoming rotund because of eating too many *Tweeback* (homemade buns) and *Schinkje Fleesch* (smoked ham), that would have been quite acceptable.

Since Diedrich chose to comment on a pregnant woman's girth, he had to be punished, but his father was charitable. He gave Diedrich permission to choose the item with which he would be spanked. It could be a leather strap, a green switch, or perhaps a dried out old stick. It was not a choice as to whether or not he would be spanked.

While he was choosing his tool of punishment, Diedrich cried miserably. He was hopeful that perhaps his father would relent if he saw how very remorseful his little boy was. It did not work. His father was determined to teach Diedrich about

manners and which things he should never, ever talk about. Diedrich may not have remembered all the social graces he was taught, but he remembered the spanking.

Jakob, Helen and Albert

Boating with the Cousins

Johan and Helena Sawatzky
|
Tina Nettie Heinrich Jakob Helena Mary Marge Anna **John** Diedrich Willie

John's aunt and uncle, Peter and Susan (*Sauntji*) Hildebrand, affectionately known as the *Sauntji* Hildebrands, lived far away from Blumenthal. They lived in Lundar, in the Interlake region of Manitoba. When John got to visit his aunt and uncle and their three boys, it seemed like an eternity to drive from Blumenthal to Lundar. Lundar was farther away than Winnipeg.

John thought it was funny that people called his uncle *Sauntji* because *Sauntji* was *Plautdietsch* for Susan and his uncle's real name was Peter. Nobody ever really called him *Sauntji* to his face. He was only referred to as *Sauntji* Hildebrand when people talked about him.

John's parents liked to visit the *Sauntji* Hildebrands because they always had fun there. John really liked to go there too because then he got to play with his cousins, whom he did not get to see nearly often enough in his opinion.

One day when John was visiting his cousins at their home near a lake, John and his three boy cousins and their dog took a rowboat out on the lake. They rowed with the clumsy wooden paddles. They rowed out far, but they could still see the pebbled shore. For John it seemed like they were very, very far from dry land. He liked to have both his lily-white feet with the chipped toenails planted firmly on the black soil.

Although it seemed far for John, his uncle and his father could easily see their sons with their rolled-up pant legs and rolled-up sleeves, handling the faded wooden rowboat on the gently rippling water. *Sauntji* Hildebrand knew that it was a good idea to watch his sons carefully, especially his son Ed, who in the past had been less than a model child.

Ed did not disappoint his father. He lived up to his father's expectations and up to his own reputation as a bad egg. Ed snatched up the dog that had

– John Sawatzky told his niece, the author, this story in July, 2001.

been innocently sitting on the boat, watching the boys row, and listening to their cajoling and giggling. With all his might, Ed hurled the dog into the water and held on to the rope that he had tied around the dog's neck.

The dog had two choices: sink or swim. He chose to swim. The dog swam ashore with the boys and the boat in tow. He arrived on the stony beach, safe and soaked, followed by the boys, who were still connected to the dog by the rope. The two stormy faced fathers had watched what was happening and they were waiting for their boys. *Sauntji* Hildebrand was very unhappy with his Ed. No sooner were Ed's feet on solid ground when his father grabbed him by his shirt sleeve and gave him a spanking that each of the boys remembered— right in front of everyone. Ed had no chance to save face. His humiliation was public.

Sketch by Katie Altendorf Cable © 2003

Justice had been done. The dog felt vindicated, but like any good dog, he would always be faithful to Ed.

Crime and Punishment

Johan M. and **Helena** Sawatzky
|
Tina Nettie Heinrich Jakob Helen Mary Marge Anna John Diedrich **Willie**

Little Willie Sawatzky loved to play in the attic—especially on rainy days when his Mama was cooking downstairs and his Papa was working in the barn beside the house. Playing in the attic felt as good as his soft flowered flannelette blanket felt when he went to sleep. In Sawatzky's home, the attic ceiling was very low. Children entered the attic through a short door. When they stood upright in the attic, they could reach up and touch the ceiling. It was perfect. It was just the right size for a small child, and the ceiling sloped so much that at its lowest point, it was the ideal height for a brown field mouse.

The attic stored many wonderful and unusual things. There were long-forgotten toys that had once been cherished and treasured by Willie's older brothers, who were now big and had left home. There were sad irons that had been heated on the stove and used to iron clothes before electric irons were invented. There were rustling brown paper bags of seeds saved from the garden, newspaper clippings, and old school notebooks with teachers' comments written with a fountain pen filled with red ink. Along one side of the wall stood an old mangle that had smoothed out wrinkled sheets and tea towels a long time ago. Along another wall was a row of bulky, heavy winter coats and woolen ski pants, waiting to be worn when the snow began to fly across the prairie landscape. Little Willie loved the mystery of the scarred toys that his older brothers and sisters had played with. He inhaled the smell of the moth-balled woolen coats. He delighted in the fragrance of the dried dill and the summer savoury that his Mama had hung from a nail against the wall. Willie knew his Mama would use the nice smelling herbs in the wintertime to flavour *Komst Borscht* (Cabbage Soup) and his favourite soup, *Riepe Schaubel Sup* (Ripe Bean Soup).

One rainy day in early autumn when Willie was playing among the winter coats, pretending that he was Robin Hood and the coats were Sherwood Forest, he came upon a treasure. It was not a pretend treasure like his pretend leafy green Sherwood Forest. It was a real treasure. The treasure was beyond Willie's wildest dreams.

– Story told to the author by her Uncle Willie, (Bill Sawatzky), on May 10, 2002 while visiting in British Columbia

Nestled in among the heavy winter coats, like a baby kitten nestled in hay, was a brand new shiny red bicycle. No one had ever used the bike—not even his just-a-little-bit-older brother Diedrich. Willie knew that for sure. The tires had no dirt on them. They smelled like the rubber tires in the store where they sold brand new shiny black cars. How could there be a bicycle in the house without him knowing about it? His Mama and Papa knew how badly he wanted a bicycle. He had told them so many, many times. Why would they keep such a secret from him? Maybe not even Papa and Mama knew about the bicycle. It was perfect. It was exactly the bicycle he wanted. He had seen it in the fat Eaton's catalogue that had the pictures of all those wonderful toys that he wanted so much.

Willie could not wait to tell his Mama about his good fortune. He raced down the stairs to where his Mama was cooking, "*Mama, weit jie waut ekj jefunge haw* (Mama do you know what I have found)?" he asked his mother, his eyes sparkling. The breathless words, telling his mother what he had found, gushed out of his entire body. He did not know how he could be so lucky.

His Mama did not look happy. Why wasn't she excited too? With a stony face and pursed lips she accused her little boy "*Ekj woa Papa saje daut dü no Wienachts Jeschenkje jeschneppat hast* (I'll tell Papa that you snooped for Christmas presents)." What was his mother saying? She was accusing him of snooping. He had not snooped. He had really found the bicycle accidentally. Willie pleaded "*Ekj deid nicht schneppre* (I did not snoop)." Willie's pleas fell upon deaf ears.

Willie's Mama and Papa knew their young boy was a curious, sneaky little fellow. Their Willie had snooped, and for what he had done, he had to be punished. Snooping, and then lying about it, was doubly wrong. The only remedy for such bad behaviour was a spanking. Their little Willie was sweet as apple pie, but the only way he could ever have found the bicycle would have been by snooping. They had hidden it ever so carefully and cleverly among the coats where Willie had no business being. They would have to punish their Willie. It was the right thing to do.

"Wash Day" by Mary Elias © 1997 by Pembina Threshermans Museum

Cooking and Cleaning

A woman's work is never done.

During the week, the Sawatzky girls churned butter in a big wooden churn. On Saturdays their father, Johan M. delivered the butter to Gallant's store in Letellier. Johan M. traded the butter for goods that they could not make or grow on the farm. He came home with armloads of sugar, yeast, baking powder, and the odd bung of bologna as a special treat.

On Saturdays, the women baked large pans of buns, loaves of bread, and one big pan of cake to be served on Sunday when they might have *Jast* (guests) come over for *Faspa*. In the winter, bread was baked indoors. In the summer, the baking was done outside in the brick bake oven. The aroma of the freshly baked bread was as welcoming as a warm handshake.

Every day except Sunday was a workday. Saturdays were especially busy in preparation for Sundays so that on Sundays, the women only needed to set the table with the food they had already prepared the day before.

Laundry Day at the Sawatzky's

Johan M. and Helena Sawatzky
|
Tina Nettie Heinrich Jakob **Helen Mary Marge Anna** John Diedrich Willie

Laundry was a huge production that happened every two weeks in the Sawatzky household. It started very early in the morning when the *Miagrope* (a large cast-iron cauldron set on a brick and mortar fireplace) was filled with water. The cavity under the *Miagrope* was filled with firewood to heat the water. The *Miagrope* was refilled with water three times to heat enough water to wash and rinse the family's piles of dirty laundry.

The whites, the coloured things, and the dark fabrics were sorted into separate heaps. A woman's worth was measured by the whiteness of her white laundry. If a man's shirt was not as white as the driven snow, or as smoothly pressed as a page in the Bible, then that was a sign that his wife was a little sloppy. Helena Sawatzky and her girls did not want to be known as sloppy.

The girls bailed the hot water from the *Miagrope* into the washing machine with the enamel bucket. The detergent, made of irregular shaped homemade lye soap bars, was shredded and added to the hot water. The first load—the white load of Sunday shirts, tea towels, handkerchiefs and undergarments—was stuffed into the washing machine. The girls took turns rocking the washing machine by pushing and pulling the wooden handle to agitate the greyed and stained laundry to a pure white.

Helena's girls, Tina, Nettie, Helen, Mary, Marge, and Anna all had to pitch in on the work. They washed the clothes until not a trace of dirt could be seen. They put soaking wet clothes through a wringer to squeeze out as much water as possible. Then the white things were put into a rinse of bleach water, followed by a rinse of bluing to make them as white as freshly fallen snow in the late afternoon. When the sun shone, all the laundry was hung outdoors on a long wire line with wooden clothespins.

White shirts, crisp blouses, and doilies needed to be starched. Helen mixed flour, a pinch of sugar, and water in a pot. She brought the mixture to a boil

Sketch by Katie Altendorf Cable © 2003

on the kitchen stove that was still hot from making the morning breakfast coffee. The starch mixture thickened to the consistency of chocolate pudding. Helen diluted the solution by adding it to a large, round zinc tub half filled with water. She dipped the Sunday shirts and things that required the extra crispness into the starch and water mixture, wrung them out, and hung them on the clothesline to dry in the warm Manitoba sun. After the sun dried the starched shirts, they could almost stand on their own.

On rainy or on cold and snowy days, the laundry was hung on lines strung up in the girls' bedrooms. Anna and Marge grew accustomed to long johns reaching down to tickle their faces as they lay in their beds, but they never got accustomed to the high humidity. It felt as if they were in a steam bath that lasted far too long.

Laundry was an all day affair. There was a lot to wash. The little children in the family created mountains of laundry. One little one in particular made sure that his sisters had plenty of diapers and clothes to wash. His sisters were not pleased with all the work he made for them, but he didn't mind.

Even though laundry was a full day's work, the girls still had meals to cook and other daily chores to do. They had to prepare the noon meal for the men folk who were working outside on the fields and for the children who were very busy making roads in the dirt with the little wooden trucks they had found in their Christmas bowl the previous Christmas. The family was accustomed to eating at noon, and they were hungry because breakfast had been very early. The noon meal was a big, heavy meal. The laundry-day menu was always the same. It was boiled navy beans, fried smoked farmer sausage or *Schinkje Fleesch* (smoked ham), and *Schmaunt Fat* (cream gravy). The beans could boil while the girls did the laundry and all that they needed to remember was: "Don't salt the beans before they are nice and soft."

The day after wash day was ironing day. What a heap of clothes there was to iron! The girls had to iron the men's shirts, pants that were as stiff as the horses' reins, embroidered tea towels with crocheted trim, the girls' dresses, and the flowered aprons that they wore to keep their dresses clean.

There were no electric irons. The iron was a handle with several sad irons that were heated on the stove. Tina licked her finger and quickly touched the iron. If it sizzled, it was hot enough to iron the clothes. If Tina hissed an "*Oi weh*," it was a sign that her finger hadn't been quick enough to leave the hot iron surface.

The sad iron was attached to the handle and the girls ironed with it until it cooled. The cooled iron was exchanged for a second iron, which was heating on the woodstove. So it went until the mountain of clothes was ironed.

Ironing the starched clothes was no easy matter. Helen lightly sprinkled the clothes with water,

rolled them up like a jellyroll, and let them soften for a few hours before they were unrolled and pressed with the iron.

Ironing was a shared job. Several girls ironed at once. They chatted, gossiped and sang together. It was hard work, but it was communal work. They shared the load and made it lighter.

Washing machine

Olga and Tina's Laundry Day

Peter S. and **Katharina** Hildebrand

|

Katharina (Tina) Maria **Olga** Helen Anna Peter Abram Henrietta Henry **Eva**

A big barn with a hayloft perfect for barn dances stood on the Edenthal farm. A row of trees guarding the farm pond provided the farmhouse beside the barn with little protection from the fierce northern winter winds that swept across the naked prairie fields.

The wooden two-storey house had not seen a paintbrush in years. It had several rooms, but not a single room had cupboards or sinks to designate it as a kitchen or a bathroom. The building was wind-proofed and insulated with sawdust-plastered wooden slats. For six years, Peter S. and Katharina Hildebrand's two daughters, Katharina (Tina) and Olga, lived in the house with their husbands and their infants. The house had been vacant before the young couples moved in.

There was water in the pond, but Olga and Tina were not equipped to do laundry in their house. They didn't have a large *Miagrope* (cast-iron cauldron set on a brick-and-mortar fireplace) in which to heat the water, or enough large tubs in which to scrub, soak and rinse their babies' dirty diapers. Their mother lived nearby, and she had all the right things needed to do laundry. Olga and Tina liked to do their laundry at their mother's.

On wash days, the two sisters gathered their laundry. They packed up all their dirty clothes, towels and sheets into bundles and stuffed them into an old yellow straw carriage that had been handed down to them from their Aunt Elizabeth and Uncle Dave Doerksen. They wheeled their laundry to their mother's place.

Two infants snuggled comfortably between the laundry bundles in the straw carriage. One child reluctantly walked with the women.

The two infants delighted in the ride. The laundry bundles cushioned them from the bumpy ride while their mothers took turns pushing the carriage. The carriage had high spoked rear wheels and matching, but smaller, spoked wheels in the front. The children giggled and napped on the roller-coaster-like ride as their mothers pushed the carriage along the dirt road with its lumpy mud clods and gopher holes.

The walk was long for all of them, especially when the strong Manitoba winds blew the black prairie dust into their faces. They walked along the lane from their house, a half-mile south on the mile road, one-mile west on the Post Road, and a half-mile south down the lane to their parents' house.

By the time Olga and Tina got to their parents' place, their mother already had all the laundry facilities set up. She had set out the tub, heated the water in the cast-iron *Miagrope* and shredded the homemade soap bars into very fine bits.

As soon as the young mothers arrived at their destination, their children scrambled to play with their Aunt Eva, who was their age. The mothers did not worry about who would mind the children while they worked. Their children would let them know when they needed to be nursed, fed, have their diapers changed, or have an "owie" kissed away.

Katharina and Olga wasted no time in attacking their laundry. Since their mother had already made all the preparations, they went directly to soaking, scrubbing, rinsing and hanging the laundry on the line with their mother's wooden clothespins. They worked quickly. They wanted to have the laundry hanging in the warm sun and gentle breeze early in the day. That way, the laundry would be dry before it was time to take the long walk home. They loved to go home with the yellow straw carriage filled with folded, fresh smelling, air-dried diapers, undergarments, aprons, dresses, socks, trousers and shirts, and three not-so-clean children.

At the end of the day, when the young women walked home, their children were tired and so were they. They had put in a full day's work and they had spent the day with their mother. The walk home was a quiet one. The infants, snuggled in the carriage, were breathing deeply and sleeping before they reached the end of the half-mile lane. The toddler, who had to walk, wanted to be in the carriage too. There was no room in the carriage for him, but every now and then, one of the young mothers picked him up and carried him home. He liked that.

Katharina's Bake Oven

Peter S. and **Katharina** Hildebrand

Like all the other farm women in rural southern Manitoba, Katharina had an outdoor clay bake oven. She baked for her ten children, for any visitors who dropped in unannounced, and for everyone helping on the farm.

The bake oven was built under the chokecherry trees that grew between the pond, where the cows languished on hot summer afternoons, and the two-story farmhouse, where Katharina and her husband Peter raised their family. Sheets of tin covered the clay bake oven to protect it from erosion by the wind and the rain.

When Katharina baked, the fire cavity under the space where the bread baked was filled with flax straw and a few dry sticks. Katharina lit the flax. It heated the oven and kindled the dried wood to which more wood was added. Soon the oven was hot enough to bake the bread that Katharina had kneaded and shaped into loaves. To keep the oven at just the right temperature Katharina and her children added wood to the stove to keep it hot for as long as the bread was baking.

Katharina did not need a thermometer to tell her when the oven was hot enough to bake bread. To determine if the oven was the right temperature to bake the risen loaves she stuck her hand into the oven. If she could not hold her hand in the oven to a count of ten, then the oven was hot enough to bake bread.

Katharina baked twenty-four loaves of bread each week. By the time a new week rolled around, there were only crumbs left in the breadbox from the previous baking. There were a lot of hungry mouths to feed in her family and, in the Hildebrand tradition, the table was always extended to more people than just the immediate family. Those people were friends, relatives, extra farm hands who helped with the harvest, or one of the children's friends who needed a place to stay for a time.

– Story told to the author by her Aunt Olga, March 25, 2002

Many hungry and grateful people enjoyed Katharina's bread. Each week the loaves of bread came out of the oven with a golden-brown crusty top. Their insides were light as a cloud and melted in your mouth. The bread was so delicious, many people had second or third slices even after their hunger had vanished. Katharina's bread was just too wonderful to stop eating after only one slice.

Sketch by Katie Altendorf Cable © 2003

Helena's Bread Making

Johan M. and **Helena** Sawatzky

Helena kneaded the dough for her homemade loaves and buns of white bread in her large enamel *Däjch Komm* (dough bowl). She set the *Däjch Komm* on the varnished wooden chair with the carved back, so that she could lean over it to knead the dough.

Before she mixed the yeast, the lard, the water, the salt, and the flour, she wrapped a kerchief around her head. She carefully tied the kerchief behind her neck, making sure that no stray hair could fall into the dough. While she kneaded, she sang her favourite hymns, *So Nimm dann meine Hände* (Take Thou my Hand O Father) and *Welch ein Treuer Freund ist Jesu* (What a Friend We Have in Jesus). They were songs that she had sung in church since she was a little girl. Helena sang song after song in her nasal voice, filling the kitchen with comfortable music.

Helena's grandchildren loved to hear her sing. Her singing was gentle and familiar like a soft and faded blanket. While their grandma sang, the children stayed near her, quietly playing with their toys and listening to their grandma's sacred music as she prepared the bread that she would break with her family.

Fresh bread (courtesy of Helena's daughter, Anna Hildebrand)

Jams for the Winter

Peter S. and **Katharina** Hildebrand

|

Katharina Mary Olga Helen Anna Peter Abram Henrietta Henry Eva

– Story told to the author by her Aunt Olga, October 26, 2002

As soon as fruit was mature, Katharina and her daughters turned it into jam. They cooked rhubarb jam in the early spring, chokecherry jam later in summer, and wild plum jam in early autumn. All the fruit grew on their Edenburg farm.

The girls washed the fruit, put it into the large navy enamel pot with the white specks, and added half as much sugar as fruit pulp. They boiled the fruit and sugar for one hour, stirring it all the while to make sure that the jam did not scorch. The jam thickened from the natural fruit pectin as it boiled. When the hour of cooking was up, the girls poured the jam into heavy stone crocks with the red wings painted on the outside and stored it in the cool basement. The preserved crocks of jam should last the family for the winter months. All winter long, whenever the jam dish needed replenishing, jam

Modern day pantry filled with preserves
(courtesy of Anna Hildebrand)

was scooped out of a stone crock into one of Katharina's pretty bowls with a picture of a woman wearing a long bustled skirt and carrying a parasol.

By January the jam, which had only half as much sugar as was needed for proper preservation, started to smell a bit like wine in its early fermentation stages. The family may have enjoyed fermented fruit in the form of wine, but it certainly did not taste good on their *Tweeback* (homemade buns). The jam remaining in the stone crock was returned to the large cooking pot, more sugar was added, and the jam was boiled again. The jam was renewed and good. It had no hint of wine flavour and the family had enough jam to last them until spring, when the first stocks of rhubarb would be long enough to transform into jam for yet another season.

Winter Preparations

Johan M. and **Helena** Sawatzky
|
Tina Nettie Heinrich Jakob Helena Mary Marge Anna John Diedrich Willie

Towards the end of the long hot summer, Helena and her daughters and any helpers she could conscript, preserved foods for the winter table. Fruit and vegetables never tasted as good in the wintertime as they did when they were freshly picked, but Helena did her best to stretch some of summer's bounty into winter. Her girls cut up chunks of garden-grown watermelons, rind and all, and pickled them. Sometimes they put whole watermelons into the pickling brine. They preserved the watermelons, covered in brine, in a large wooden barrel. To preserve the fruit, they sealed the barrel filled with watermelons and brine, with melted paraffin wax. The family could look forward to munching on sweet-and-sour crunchy watermelons to accompany their meals throughout the long cold winter.

Large cucumbers were picked from the vine. They were preserved with dilled salty brine in a separate wooden barrel. At the end of the cucumber season, all the little cucumbers still clinging to the vine were picked and pickled in sweet brine with homegrown cauliflower. The sweet pickles were stored in stone crocks and saved for winter meals around a warm table while the wind was raging outdoors.

To ensure there would be very little risk of any food going bad, all the cucumber pickles had to be eaten before the watermelon barrel's wax seal was cracked.

Pickled cucumbers and pickled watermelons were a small fraction of the preserving that the Sawatzky girls did. The family needed a lot of jam. They ate jam for breakfast, jam for *Faspa*, and usually there was jam on the table at dinner and supper. The girls made rhubarb jam, plum jam, Saskatoon (usually called blueberry) jam, and chokecherry jam. All the fruit was grown on the farm except the Saskatoons, which grew wild in the bushes in *Jantsied* (other side, referring to the other side of the Red River). The jam was stored in large stone crocks. In the wintertime, the jam was spooned out of the crocks into small dishes and set on the table. To make small pints of jam for families as large as thirteen or more was a waste of time and a huge waste of little jars.

There was another job besides food preparation that had to be done during the summer. The children had to prepare firewood to heat the houses in the wintertime. Their father and big brother cut firewood in the bushes in *Jantsied*. The children had to collect cow patties (also known as cow pies) and turn them over to dry in the summer heat. Once they were dry and firm like paper boxes from the store, they stacked and stored the patties for additional fuel to heat the house during the wintertime.

Every family member who was old enough to work, worked hard to prepare for winter. The summer was short, and much work had to be completed before the arrival of winter's freezing winds and snowdrifts.

By the time winter was over and spring rolled around again, many families appreciated new variety in their diet. In the springtime, a cheese peddler traveled from farmhouse to farmhouse peddling a big round of cheese. Whenever the peddler arrived at the Sawatzky home, Johan Sawatzky bought a big chunk of cheese from him. He bought enough cheese to feed his family and enough cheese to treat their *Jast* (guests) for Sunday's *Faspa*. It was a real treat after a winter of preserved and pickled foods.

Sketch by Katie Altendorf Cable © 2003

Prips

Peter S. and **Katharina** Hildebrand
|
Katharina Maria Olga Helen Anna Peter Abram Henrietta Henry Eva

– Information given to the author by her Aunt Olga

Prips was the beverage of choice for most Mennonite families during the Depression of the 1930s when there was no cash to buy coffee. Some folks acquired quite a taste for the hot drink.

To make a cup of *Prips* was a lot more labour intensive than opening a can of ground coffee and letting the coffee maker do the work. *Prips* was made from the barley grown on the farm and stored in the granary. The women and their daughters cleaned the barley of all the dirt, thistle weeds, and grasshopper body parts. They washed the grain to be sure that it was perfectly clean. They dried the grain in the oven that was at a very low temperature. After the grain was dry, the oven was stoked to raise the temperature in order to toast the barley. The women watched the roasting barley closely, because it scorched very easily, and *Prips* made from burned barley was not something anyone wanted to drink.

The roasted barley was ground in a manually operated coffee grinder screwed onto a wooden beam. When the *Prips* was prepared, one and one half cups of roasted ground barley was added to twelve cups of boiling water. The problem was that once the barley was boiled, it expanded like a pot of boiling porridge, and twelve cups of water did not yield a lot of *Prips*.

Prips was usually served at breakfast, and at *Faspa* along with homemade buns and jam. It tasted best when rich cream was added to the hot cups of *Prips*.

Katharina Hildebrand always offered cream when she served *Prips*—except for one winter when there was no cream for her to offer. The feed for the cows was so poor, that the cows gave no milk and a few pregnant cows died that year. Everyone in the district was poor, and all the fathers and mothers worried about how they would put food into their children's stomachs, never mind cream for *Prips*. They worried, and they struggled, but they survived. They were creative and resourceful people.

War and Peace

"The Depression, followed by the Second World War, brought changes which left their mark on the community. Another generation of young men went off to war…This time more Mennonite men joined the armed forces, despite the pacifist teachings of their church."

F. G. Enns, 1987
Gretna, Window on the Northwest, Page 286

One of the tenets of the Mennonite faith, that separates it from other Christian faiths, is that Mennonites are pacifists. When young Mennonite men enlisted in the military, it was exceptionally difficult for their parents. The parents worried for the safety of their sons fighting in a far-off land and they worried that their sons were not practicing the pacifism of the Mennonite faith. The parents also had to face the disapproval of their Mennonite friends and neighbours at home.

My Boys are Doing Good

Peter S. and **Katharina** Hildebrand
|
Katharina Maria Helen Olga Anna **Peter Abram** Henrietta Henry Eva

Peter S. Hildebrand had just received the worst blow in his life. His firstborn, also named Peter, had just announced that he had enlisted in the army. The senior Peter's heart weighed upon his chest like a cold blade of steel. Ever since he had become a father of sons, he had pleaded with his God to protect his boys from the horrors of war. Now his son had enlisted on his own free will. He did not want to lose his sons. He wanted to keep them at home and safe on the farm. It was against all his values and against the beliefs of his church to go to war. As a Mennonite, he was a pacifist and his sons should be too. They should be conscientious objectors just like many of the other Mennonite boys.

"Wuaromm säjst dü mie nijch waut dü em Senn haudst

(Why did you not tell me what your intentions were)?" the senior Peter asked his young son. "Because you would have talked me out of it," was the young man's response.

On the day of young Peter's departure, his father took him to board the train in Emerson where he was scheduled to catch the first leg of his long journey to Europe to fight for freedom and peace. It was a quiet trip. Neither father nor son had the words to say what was in their hearts. They commented on the ripening crops and wished for good weather, but words of worry and love were silenced by their tightened throats and misted eyes. Only when the young Peter boarded the train could his father wrestle words from his soul. He called after his boy, *"Peta* (Peter)". He hesitated a moment, shuffled

Faspa — 146 — A Snack of Mennonite Stories

– Story told to the author by her Uncle Peter Hildebrand on November 10, 2002.

his feet on the wooden station platform worn from many shoes, and quietly cautioned his son, "Don't get hooked up with any German prostitutes." The young Peter had no idea that his father knew about such things. He listened to his father and saved his little smile until after the train began chugging towards Winnipeg.

To make matters even more horrible for Peter S. and Katharina, their second son Abram also enlisted in the army. Peter S. and Katharina spent many sleepless nights, praying for the safety of their sons fighting in a distant war. Unlike many non-Mennonite families who received an abundance of support from their friends and neighbours when their sons were overseas, Peter S. and Katharina got no support. Other families who had sons fighting in the war were proud of their sons. Peter S.'s. heart felt like a cold piece of lead in his chest. He was not proud that his sons went to fight overseas—except when he went to the post office in Gretna. That was the one time and the one place where he got support.

He went to the Gretna post office regularly to pick up his mail. Each time he went into the post office, the postmaster, Charlie Hayward, asked, "Well, Peter, how are the boys doing?" Peter's eyes sparkled just a little, thinking of his brave sons. He slowly took another puff from his smoke and tobacco stained pipe, and replied, "My boys are doing good." For just a brief moment, the senior Peter's chest got a little bit bigger, and he stood just a little bit taller.

The Telegram

Peter S. and **Katharina** Hildebrand

|

Tina Maria Helen Olga Anna **Peter** Abram Henrietta Henry Eva

Every family has stories that are told over and over again. Sometimes children hear the stories so often, they are not sure whether they remember the stories or whether they only remember what they've been told by their aunts, uncles, parents, and grandparents.

Every family also has stories that are remembered by a few witnesses and never talked about—or not talked about for many years. Each person who was present when the story occurred remembers the incident in his or her own way.

Katharina Hildebrand's grandchildren all remembered being told that Katharina had turned from a carrot-topped red-head to a grey-haired lady during the years her sons Peter and Abram were fighting overseas. The children were told of their grandmother turning grey, and they were told about how some people from their church refused to talk with their grandparents during that time, but they were never told of how painful that time was for Katharina.

Katharina and her husband Peter S. had been away visiting relatives when the telegram was delivered to the frame farmhouse half a mile south of the Post Road. The telegram was received by their teenaged children, who left the paper on the kitchen table for their parents to see when they arrived home.

During the war years, telegrams were always harbingers of sorrow. They never brought joy. The telegram delivered to the Hildebrand farm was no exception. Peter S. and Katharina's first born son Peter was missing in action.

The senior Peter put the paper back on the table. He could not read English well, but he understood this message, and he knew that "Missing in Action" meant that he would never see his namesake again. He paced all night. His son was undoubtedly lying on foreign land, thousands of miles away. Why had he said to his Peter, "I would rather bury you in the cemetery than take you to the train that will deliver you to the European conflict?" He didn't

– Story told to the author by her father, Henry D. Hildebrand, in July, 2000, when they were celebrating his 73rd birthday at the Kam Loon Restaurant in Morris, Manitoba.

want his son dead. He wanted him alive and at home. He wanted to hold him like he had when his son was a squirming infant. He loved Peter as only a father can love a son—with all his heart and soul.

Katharina paced only for a little while. Then she sat down in the rocking chair in which she had nursed her beautiful baby who was now missing in action. She sat in that rocking chair day after day, rocking, week after week, rocking. She said nothing—she could not cry. There were no tears. There were never tears for Katharina. The pain was jailed inside her body. It could go nowhere. It only screamed inside her. She wept without tears. Her whole body wept.

As she sat and rocked, week after week, her back got more curved, the lines in her face got deeper, and her autumn, carrot-topped red-head, turned to winter. The snow on her head stayed. Katharina could not imagine that joy would ever revisit her.

Joy, however, did return. Months later, news came from overseas. Peter was no longer missing in action. He was recovering in hospital in England. No news could have been more welcome. Katharina and Peter S. celebrated their good fortune. Each gave thanks in their own way, but the scar left by the pain of the telegram never disappeared.

Peter Hildebrand (courtesy of Peter and Doris Hildebrand)

Meeting the Train

Peter S. and Katharina Hildebrand
|
Katharina Maria Helen Olga Anna **Peter** Abram **Henrietta Henry Eva**

It was October 31, 1945. The conflict in Europe had been over for a good number of months, and families were impatiently waiting for their boys to come home. The Hildebrands were celebrating for more reasons than many families were. Not only one, but two of their boys, Abram (also known as Alan) and Peter, were coming home. The family would not have to visit the crosses, row on row, to find a cross bearing one of their son's or brother's name. This meeting would be so powerful and close to the heart because months earlier, their father, Peter S. Hildebrand had received the most dreaded and feared telegram, advising him, "Your son Peter Hildebrand is missing in action." A subsequent and much more welcome communiqué told the family that Peter had indeed been missing in action and that he was convalescing in a British hospital.

The Hildebrand family, who lived over sixty miles south of Winnipeg, had been told that Peter's troop, the Fort Garry Horse, would be arriving in Winnipeg the very next day. The senior Peter hired one of the Hruda boys, the neighbour's son, to take his youngest son, who had been too young to fight for his country, and three of his daughters to greet the train that his namesake would be arriving on. The senior Peter knew that he would not be able to hide the emotion he would feel upon greeting his son. His pride would not allow him to show those feelings in a place as public as the railway station. What if he cried? What would he say to the son whom he had taken to a much smaller railway station and said good-bye to, years earlier?

He would rather let his young son and his daughters go to meet Peter. It didn't matter if they cried or laughed; after all, they were young. Henry, Henrietta, Eva and Anna took the long trip into Winnipeg to see their handsome brother for the first time in years.

The young people could not wait to see the brother they had missed so much. The conversation between them moved from what it would be like to see Peter again, to moments of silence. Each of the four youths had their own memories of what it was like at home without him. Henrietta remembered only too vividly how she was the one who had to walk the five miles to Gretna to advise the post-master, Mr. Haywood, that the family had received the telegram saying Peter was missing in action. Those were five miles of walking on broken glass for Henrietta. Now she would see the same brother who had been missing.

Eva thought about the day she had found her parents sitting in the living room and they told her Peter and her other brother Abram were going to war. Little Eva asked her parents when her brothers would come back home. Her parents only looked at her with their sad eyes and remained silent. Anna and Henry had their thoughts too, but they just wanted to see Peter and they could not get to the big train station in Winnipeg fast enough for their liking.

Peter had his own moments of wondering what it would be like to be back home after all that he had seen in the European conflict. What would it be like to see his brother who was probably shaving by now? When the young Peter had left home, Eva was still a skinny little girl with no hips. Now she was a young woman. No one had prepared him for the changes he would see in his little sister.

The train station was decorated to give the young men a hero's welcome. The walkway from the train platform to the station exit was cordoned off with sturdy rope. The band was poised to play. The train chugged into the station. For the eager crowd, it came to a stop painstakingly slowly. When the door of the passenger cars opened, pandemonium broke out. The band played, the crowds screamed, cried, shouted, and laughed amongst streams of ticker tape. Everyone craned to see his or her own loved one.

Eva was the first sister to sight Peter. She screamed "Peter" and ran to him, embracing her big brother in a way that only a little sister can. She had worried about him and missed him terribly. Peter was home at last.

Over fifty years later, Henrietta told this story as if it happened the day before. Her skin still shivered with goose bumps, remembering the tide of emotion of that moment. She fought back her tears remembering that day, that train station, and that once-in-a-lifetime greeting that happened so long ago.

Memories

Peter S. and Katharina Hildebrand
|
Katharina Maria Helen Olga Anna Peter **Abram (Alan)** Henrietta Henry Eva

---

Remembrance Day is an important day. There was a time when November 11th was referred to as Armistice Day. Armistice Day was the day that ended hostilities in the First World War of 1914-1919. A time to remember. A time to forget.

Only once did Alan ever talk about his participation as a young foot soldier in World War II. Only once did he talk about the cruelties of war. Even that one time, he spoke as if he had not been there—as if he was talking about someone else. He talked about a hill that he and his comrades were on. It was as though he had not been there when he spoke of the twelve-year old German boys firing at the young Canadian soldiers. It was as though he had not been there when he and his comrades had to protect themselves from the children bearing arms. Then he quickly changed the subject. He never forgot.

Years later, when November 11th, the time to remember or to forget, came around again, as it had for so many years before, a niece asked him,

"Uncle Al, will you be going to the Remembrance Day ceremonies?" His only reply…"No, I don't go anymore. It just makes me cry."

Alan Hildebrand

The Ration Book

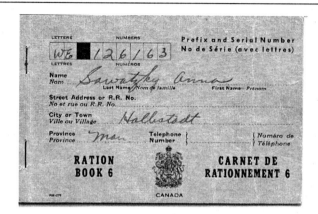

Ration book (courtesy of Anna Hildebrand, nee Sawatzky)

During World War II, Gasoline License and Ration Coupon Books were issued to individuals to buy rationed products. The conditions under which the coupons could be used, were posted in the coupon books in both English and French. People were urged to take their Ration Books with them when they traveled because they were good anywhere in Canada. The Ration Books were issued by the Ration Administration – Wartime Prices and Trade Board, Box 250, Station "B", Montreal. The books were intended to ration supplies that were needed but were not always readily available. Such supplies were butter, sugar, and gasoline, to name a few. The Ration Book had pages of little coupons in it and each coupon made the Ration Book owner eligible to purchase the product indicated on the coupon by a letter. For example, when someone bought butter, the buyer gave the shopkeeper butter coupons with a large "B" and a number on it, along with money to pay for the butter. The shopkeeper was accountable for the ration coupons and the rations that he sold. If a Ration Book owner used up all the coupons before new Ration Books were issued, the owner had to go without that product until the new Ration Books came out.

Of course, there were ways of getting more product than one was rationed. There was the situation where two young fellows went out in the one fellow's car. The boys did not have enough gasoline to go where they wanted to go and they had no gasoline coupons permitting them to buy more gasoline. The fellows were undaunted. They knew how to get additional gasoline without coupons and without stealing. They knew that a

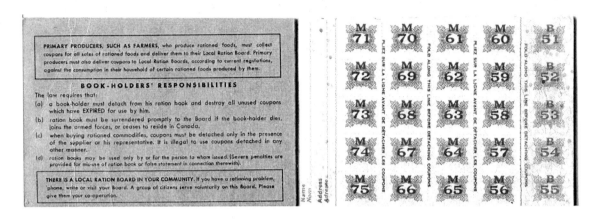

Ration coupons (courtesy of Anna Hildebrand, nee Sawatzky)

certain gentleman in their district was a kind man who also had some extra gasoline. The two fellows drove almost up to that certain gentleman's yard, and pretended that for some odd reason their car had stalled there. The car still had some gasoline in the tank, but they needed more. They were smart enough in the ways of vehicles to turn the ignition key and make the car sound as though it was refusing to start. They kept turning the ignition key so that it would sound as though they were trying to start the car. The car did not start.

The gentleman went to see what the fellows were up to and to find out what was wrong with the car and why it did not start. Just as the boys had hoped, he determined that the car needed gasoline. The gentleman was pleased to help the boys out of their predicament. He went to his gasoline storage, and brought the fellows enough gasoline to get their car started and then some. The boys were delighted. They had enough gasoline to go to town and they did not use any gasoline coupons.

Love and Marriage

First Comes Love
Then Comes Marriage

Marriages took place between two people in love. In Mennonite communities, it was thought to be a good thing when the two people in love came from the same district. That way, both partners could be close to their families and get the support they needed. It was definitely good if their families attended the same church. Mixed marriages between couples from different sectors of the Mennonite churches were of concern to families. The more liberal churches saw the conservative Mennonite churches as somewhat staid and backwards. The conservative churches saw the liberal churches as worldly and not particularly grounded in the true faith. People were judged by their church affiliation and it was good to stay within one's own church.

Johan's Ukrainian Wedding

Johan M. and Helena Sawatzky
|
Tina **Nettie** Heinrich **Jakob** Mary Marge Anna John Diedrich Willie

---

Johan and Helena were invited to a Ukrainian wedding reception in Caliento, a little Ukrainian district nestled in the wooded southeast corner of Manitoba. Johan said it was in *Jantsied* (the other side, a term used by the Mennonites when referring to the other side of the Red River).

Johan had heard that Ukrainian weddings went on for three days and that the bride kissed all the guests. He had heard that there was enough alcohol served at a Ukrainian wedding to float the Titanic. He had heard that the male guests threw the groom up into the air, turned him upside down so that all his money would fall out of his pockets, and then they presented him to the bride with his emptied pockets. All this made Johan curious enough to accept the invitation to the wedding reception.

On the morning of the wedding reception, Johan and Helena packed their Model T car with as many of their children as the car could hold, and motored to Caliento. Johan sat behind the steering wheel, wearing his Sunday hat, and Helena sat in the front seat on the woman's side, wearing her Sunday dress with the sparkly brooch. Their children, Tina, Heinrich, Nettie, and Jakob sat in the back seat, dressed in their Sunday clothes. Nettie could hardly wait to get to the wedding because she had heard her father mention that there would be dancing at the wedding. Nettie liked nothing better than to swing and twirl to a lively polka band.

The road to Caliento was so rugged with potholes, stones, weeds and underbrush that it felt as if they were riding a roller coaster with parts of the track missing. During the drive, Johan became a little concerned that if it was true that the bride kissed all the guests, that could mean that she might also kiss him. He loudly assured himself and his family, "*Kjeena voat mie kusse—fedolt nijch* (No one will kiss me—no darn way)." Johan had never kissed or been kissed in public. That was a private matter between him and his Helena.

As soon as Johan and his family arrived at the reception, the bride and her entourage of polka-

– Story told to the author by her Uncle Jake J. Sawatzky, Oct. 31, 2001 and her Aunt Nettie Neufeld, January 11, 2002.

playing musicians hurried out to greet them. The bride went directly to Johan and, without warning or hesitation, she smacked him right on the lips, in front of everybody. The engine of the car had not even stopped purring. Johan was speechless. His swarthy face turned as red as Helena's geraniums blooming on her windowsills. His children had never seen a stranger kiss their father, and they had never seen their father's face turn that colour.

Young Jakob was still in the back seat when he saw the strange woman kiss his father. It took every ounce of his self-control not to laugh at his father's red face and saucer-sized eyes. He had never seen his father in such a state. Oh my, this would be a wonderful story to tell his friends.

The polka band ushered the Sawatzky family into the house, where the groom hung up their coats, the bride offered them food and drink, and the bride's mother invited them to dance and to make themselves at home. Some older women were cooking potato perogies, cheese perogies, and sauerkraut perogies. They were wrapping rice in cabbage leaves, and they were rolling up cottage cheese crepes. Every now and then, they interrupted their cooking with a spirited two-step. Although it was around noon, dancing was in full swing. The band played and the dancers danced. Everything was so different from anything the children had ever seen before.

Young Nettie's dark eyes followed every move. She watched as though she was watching a many-ringed circus. Everything was happening at once. Young and old were dancing in twos, threes, or fours; food was being prepared; food was being served; drinks were being poured; and everyone was talking and laughing all at once. Everyone was so jolly.

The food was completely different from anything she had ever seen at a Mennonite wedding. The big hams, the perogies, the dill pickles, the red *Borscht*, the cabbage rolls and the sausages all looked mouth-watering. Nettie and her sister and brothers were very hungry after their long ride, and they were eager to eat the delicious smelling food. Nettie took one bite of the meaty ham and could eat no more. Everything was loaded with garlic. How could anyone eat something that tasted so awful? Nettie felt tricked. To top it all off, smack dab in the middle of the table was a bowlful of mushrooms. How could anyone eat those funny looking white things that grew out of cow pies in the fence?

The perogies looked as good as the *Werenike*, that her mother made, but they were filled with potatoes and cheese. Nettie had only ever had them filled with *Glums* (cottage cheese) and served with *Schmaunt Fat* (cream gravy). To eat perogies without *Glums* and *Schmaunt Fat* was wrong. The children could not eat the food because everything was laced with garlic. They could only feast with their eyes. They saw home brew right out on the table for all to see. At Mennonite weddings, they had only seen men drink liquor in little nips outside by their cars. Bottles were never out on tables for all to see. They were hidden and out of sight.

Around midnight, a table was set with a bowl filled with grain and a bottle of whiskey. The polka band played as the bride and groom stood behind the table. Guests lined up in front of the couple across the table from them. One by one, the guests put gifts of money for the bride and groom into the bowl. As a thank you for the gift, each guest was offered a swig of whiskey from the bottle with a kiss from the bride for all the men, and a kiss from the groom for all the women. This was far too much kissing for the Sawatzkys.

Nettie watched and watched. At the end of the day, she decided that her most favourite thing of the whole day was when two men carefully brought out a big, braided bread that looked like a fancy cake. Little dough doves were perched on the layers of bread. Nettie had never seen such pretty bread. She knew how much work it must have been to make something so fancy. She would certainly never have enough time to fiddle with little dough birds like that. She could make a nice big bun in less than half the time! Then again, she wished someone would show her how to make those cute little things. Maybe she could try making one or two birds the next time she baked bread.

The Proposal

Johan M. and Helena Sawatzky

|

Tina Nettie Heinrich Jakob Helena Mary Marge Anna John Diedrich Willie

Peter Friesen was courting Johan Sawatzky's eldest and tallest daughter, Tina. Peter only took note of Tina's height because she was substantially taller than he was. Peter was smitten and he proposed to Tina that they have a talk with her father about a lifelong union between them. Tina agreed. It was customary for the hopeful groom to formally ask the potential bride's father for his daughter's hand in marriage. Peter and Tina both knew the rule, and they made plans to approach Tina's father on a particular evening.

Peter was nervous, excited, scared, and fidgety about the task that lay ahead of him. He needed to share his nervousness. He called on his good friends, and told them of the plans that he and Tina had made.

He told Candy (John) Friesen. Candy was a young entrepreneur who went from store to store, selling chocolates and candy to the proprietors. It was only fitting that he was called Candy. Sometimes Candy even sold his products at private parties.

Perhaps he gave Tupperware the idea of private home parties. Peter also told his friend *Kjliena Fries' Beant* (little Friesen's Ben) about his plan. He told Tina's younger brother Jakob and a few more local fellows. These fellows were a lot like Peter himself. They could not let an opportunity for a good prank fall by the wayside. The boys wasted no time in putting their heads together to plan a trick on their good friend Peter.

The boys knew the lay of every house in the district. Since the time their mothers had nursed them as wee babes, they had visited and played together in each other's homes. The boys all knew the Sawatzky house where Peter would go to ask Johan Sawatzky if Tina could be his bride. The boys knew that if they looked into the window of the Sawatzky home from a safe distance of 200 feet, they would be able to see exactly when Tina and Peter entered the living room to have the big chat with Johan.

Peter had a keen sense of humour, but the task that

– Story told to the author by Tina's brother, Jake J. Sawatzky, July 14 and October 31, 2001.

he had put upon himself was frightening and not even a little funny. What he planned to do required mustering up a mountain of courage. He practiced the words: "*Oomkje Sawatzji, ekj sie jüne Mejal Tien oba sea gout* (Mr. Sawatzky, I like your girl Tina very much)" or "*Oomkje Sawatzji, wie welle onns befriee, waut denkj jie doa von?* (Mr. Sawatzky, we want to get married, what do you think about it?)"

Upon Tina and Peter's entry into the living room to meet with Tina's father, all of Peter's rehearsing and deliberating went up in smoke. From about 200 feet south of the house, they heard a shotgun fire, a seat from a plow banging against the fence, and a drill disc being beaten like a cymbal.

Although Johan Sawatzky had a marked hearing impairment, even he could hear that something serious was going on outside his house. He jumped up from his varnished rocking chair and ran to open the wooden framed window that opened to the south. He yelled out in the direction of the racket, "*Scheet nijch miene Pead en Tün* (Don't shoot my horses in the fence)." Peter knew that no one was shooting anything, especially not Johan's horses. He knew it was a troop of his rowdy friends having a great deal of fun by making things very uncomfortable for him. Peter promised himself that he would pay his friends back for this.

Maybe Peter never got around to asking Johan the all-important question, but they came to an agreement because Tina and Peter married. They kept the promise they made on their wedding day—"till death do us part". Peter regained his sense of humour and he kept his promise to play the same trick on his friends when their time came to ask for their brides' hands in marriage.

The Wedding Invitation

When a young man and a young woman planned to marry, a single hand-written invitation was circulated to all the invited guests. When Nettie Sawatzky married Peter Neufeld, one hand-written announcement said that Peter Neufeld would be married to Aganetha Sawatzky, daughter of Mr. and Mrs. Johan M. Sawatzky on July 2, 1936 at the home of the Johan M. Sawatzkys. Aganetha was her Christian name, but everyone called her Nettie.

When Anna Sawatzky married Henry Hildebrand from another district, the invitation list was subdivided into districts indicating the guests from each district

The announcement was penned in letterform in a fine script with black ink from the inkwell in Johan's writing desk. It served as the invitation to all the guests for the wedding. The announcement was placed in a paper envelope, along with a handwritten list of all the people who were invited to the occasion. The list included all the neighbours and relatives. The name of the head of the household on the list meant that the entire family was invited. For the sake of the people invited, the list was in the order of where people lived. If the next door neighbours were the John Friesens, and next to them were the Peter Bergens, then at the top of the list would be *Herr* Johann Friesen (Mr. John Friesen) and second would be *Herr* Peter Bergen (Mr. Peter Bergen). When the invitation was extended to a widow and her family, her name on the invitation list read *Witwe* Isaac Doerksen (Widow Isaac Doerksen). It was a grave social error when a neighbour was missed from the list.

The invitation was hand delivered to the John Friesens, the first household on the list, and they indicated that they had seen the invitation by making a mark next to their name on the long list of invited guests. They then delivered the invitation to the Peter Bergens, who in turn delivered it to the next people on the list.

Once an invitation was received, it was expected that the recipient pass it on to the next people on the list quickly to ensure everyone was well aware of the invitation before the wedding. It was bad manners to leave the invitation on the kitchen table and forget about it.

After the invitation was sent on its journey to family, friends, and neighbours, and before the wedding, an engagement party called a *Felafniss* was held for the betrothed couple. Everyone, who was invited to the wedding, was welcome to come to *Felafniss*. The party was a dance with lots of food and music to celebrate the engagement of a young couple

Henry and Anna Hildebrand's
wedding invitation list
(courtesy of Henry D. Hildebrand)

in love and soon to be married. Nettie Sawatzky could not wait for the *Felafniss* planned for her and Peter. On the night of her *Felafniss* she danced until there was no more music. She only wished the joy of that moment would never go away.

Peter Neufeld Marries Nettie Sawatzky – A Traditional Mennonite Wedding

Johan M. and **Helena** Sawatzky
|
Nettie

Nettie Sawatzky married Peter Neufeld on July 2, 1936. It was during the Great Depression. Food lines, unemployment, drought, and basement prices for wheat were common.

As was the custom, Nettie and Peter were married on a Thursday. Thursdays were wedding days because on Saturday people prepared for Sunday, and Sunday was a day of rest. A wedding day was not a day of rest. It was a day with a whole lot of work—especially for the women.

When Nettie was planning her wedding, she wanted to buy her dear Peter a wedding present, but she had no money. She mustered up all her courage and approached her father. She asked him, "*Doaf ekj Peta en Hamd onn en Haulsbaunt fe onse Kjast bestale* (May I order Peter a shirt and tie for our wedding)?" Nettie's father gave her permission to buy the gift for her husband-to-be. Nettie spent $5.00 on a shirt and tie that she ordered from the fat Eaton's catalogue with the corners that had been curled from wishful fingers pointing to all the wonderful things to buy.

Before the Wedding

The day before the wedding, Nettie and her sisters kneaded bread dough to be baked and served to the wedding guests. The dough was parceled off into *Kjnädsels* (large balls of dough). Each *Kjnädsel* was large enough to make several dozen buns. It was the boys' job to deliver the *Kjnädsels* to the neighbours early in the morning the day before the wedding. The neighbour women shaped buns out of the large bulk of dough and baked it in their own clay ovens. Some women rolled tiny buns and some made large round buns. No one ever knew for sure whether the small buns were so small because they could feed more people and whether the large buns were a way of saving time and energy. Certainly each woman had her own style of shaping buns. Each woman who had baked buns, brought the buns with her when she came to the wedding.

While the buns were baked at the neighbours, the loaves were baked at Nettie's home. Once the dough had risen, it was punched down, allowed to rise again, and then nimble hands shaped the dough into loaves and slapped them into large loaf pans. Once the loaves rose into nicely rounded tops, they were set in the outdoor clay bake oven, that had been heated and stoked to just the right temperature. After one hour, the loaves were pulled out of the oven. They were golden brown with crispy crusts. The aroma wafted over the yard, beckoning hungry children at play. Nettie's little brothers wanted to eat the bread immediately. They had smelled the wholesome aroma and could not wait for that first crunchy bite.

The women made most of the wedding preparations. Nettie's *Tien Mum* (Aunt Tina) and *Auntji Mum* (Aunt Anne) made the *Plüme Mooss* (Sweet Fruit Soup). *Plüme Mooss* was the tasty soup made with sugar, water, dried fruit and a little flour for thickening. It tasted best when it was served cold. The aunts made the *Mooss* in a *Miagrope* (a large cauldron set on a brick and mortar fireplace), which was stationed in the garage at the south end of the farmyard. After the *Mooss* was cooked, young Nettie carried it, enamel bucket by enamel bucket, into the cellar where it would keep cool. The cool cellar was the best, and the only refrigeration available.

The girls and the women had to make sure there were enough dishes, cutlery, and serving bowls for the big day. They cooked the food for the wedding; they swept every little dust bunny hiding under the beds; they scrubbed the floors to a waxy glow; and they made sure all the clothes for the wedding were brushed, cleaned and pressed. The boys drove about the district borrowing benches and chairs from the neighbours to make sure each guest had a place to sit at the wedding. They set up the chairs and benches inside the kitchen and outside the kitchen door under a makeshift awning for people to sit on during the wedding ceremony. The ceremony was sure to last well over an hour.

The Morning of the Wedding Day

On the day of the wedding, the final preparations started early. The *Miagrope* belly was filled with firewood to boil the beef for the Cabbage *Borscht*.

Some guests, including Peter Neufeld, Nettie's husband-to-be, and guests as far away as Winkler, over thirty miles away, arrived early enough to have breakfast with the Sawatzkys.

After breakfast, the rush began. One girl cut up the cabbage, diced the potatoes, and sliced the onions for the *Borscht*. She tossed the vegetables into the beef broth along with chopped dill and salt. Another girl laid out bologna slices and slices of roast beef on large enamel plates with roses painted on them. The other girls set the table, prepared to boil the coffee, poured thick cream into china pitchers with pictures on them of ladies with big hats and long crinolined skirts.

Even though the wedding took place in the afternoon, numerous guests were welcomed for dinner at noon. All of Peter's family came. There were Peter's parents and his fourteen brothers and sisters. Also at the dinner table were Nettie's parents with Nettie and their other eleven children. In addition, the Winkler guests, and the aunts and uncles who came to help with the preparations, naturally stayed for dinner too. A day's work was accomplished before the afternoon wedding.

Moments before the Wedding

Nettie was so busy with all the food preparation and washing the dishes that her mother had to remind her "*Mejal, woascht dü die nijch boolt fe de Kjast reed moake* (Girl, won't you soon get yourself ready for the wedding)?"

Nettie scampered up the stairs to get into the new black dress that she had purchased at Eaton's *em Kjalla* (in the basement) for the handsome sum of $3.00. She slipped her little feet into her new black shoes. It was the church tradition that the bride wore dark clothes when she exchanged wedding vows with her groom. When Nettie came downstairs dressed in black, her father looked at his daughter in black, and said *"Na, ekj wull die mol met dien Brüt Kjleet auf näme* (Well, I wanted to photograph you in your wedding dress)." He was referring to the white dress that Nettie could not wear for the wedding ceremony. The white dress was the real wedding dress that she would wear after the ceremony and during the evening celebrations.

Nettie raced back upstairs, forgetting her elegant composure on the bottom stair. She changed into her new white dress and new white shoes. She pinned on her corsage of velvety fabric flowers with the long pastel ribbons that flowed to her waist. She glided down the stairs, feeling so pretty. She and Peter went to the garden to pose for her father's camera. Nettie was so lovely and so full of joy. This was truly her day and Peter's day.

Nettie knew she had to get back into her new black dress and black shoes before she and Peter exchanged their vows in front of all the guests and before the minister, *Oomkji Kjliena Friese* (Mr. Little Friesen). Her grandfather caught a glimpse of her in her white dress before she could change back into her black clothes. He approached her with a disapproving *"So west dü die trüe lote* (Is that how you want to let yourself be married)?" meaning, "Is that how you will be dressed when you get married?" Nettie responded with a *"Na, nä* (well no)" just as quickly and hurried upstairs to get back into black.

Her mother had sewn her white wedding dress. This was out of the ordinary because her mother generally left the sewing to her daughters. Nettie had intended to sew her own dress, but she had just been too busy to sew. Her mother had been worried that Nettie might not get around to sewing her dress, so one day while Nettie was out with Peter visiting neighbours, as was customary for an engaged couple, her mother tackled the job. Nettie's mother was not an accomplished seamstress, but she tried. When her mother said to Nettie "*Ekj ha die en Brüt Kjleet jeneit* (I've sewn you a bride dress)," Nettie could not imagine what sort of pattern and fabric her mother had chosen without Nettie's advice.

It was indeed a white dress, but her mother had misjudged the length of the front and back gores. She had simply patched pieces where she had cut the fabric too short and then camouflaged the unwanted seams with ruffles. The neckline also had a few ruffles around it and the dress was sleeveless except for ruffles sewn around the armholes. Nettie suspected her mother had not wanted to sew sleeves because they demanded extra work and precision.

The Wedding

Finally it was 2:00 p.m. and time to exchange vows. Nettie and Peter promised themselves to each other for the rest of their lives in front of their families, friends, and neighbours who had come, with all their children in tow, to celebrate this blessed event.

The wedding took place in the kitchen of the two-room Sawatzky house. The minister, *Oomkji Kjliena Friese*, and Peter and Nettie were in the kitchen with as many guests as the room could hold. The other guests were seated on chairs and benches outside under the *Schaute Dack* (shade roof) on the east side of the house where the kitchen door opened to the outside. This door was only ever used when there was a wedding in the household. It could have been called the wedding door.

The length of the wedding ceremony depended on the preacher. Peter and Nettie chose *Oomkji Kjliena Friese* to marry them because his services were shorter than most. His motto was that if he saw one person glancing at his watch, it was time to put an end to his preaching.

After the service, everyone was served *Faspa* (coffee and snack time between lunch and supper). All the women and girls old enough to help, pitched in. *Tien Mum* and *Auntji Mum* were assigned the job of brewing coffee in the *Miagrope*. All the buns that had been baked in the neighbouring clay bake ovens were put into serving bowls and put on the tables. The tables were set with store bought Village cookies (also known as Baby cookies), gingersnaps, marshmallow cookies, fresh dill pickles, sugar cubes, and thick farm cream for the coffee. Adults *spatseared* (visited) over *Faspa*. The children played tag, Anti Anti-Over, and Hide-and-Go-Seek. The young women and girls washed the dishes and reset the tables because, with so many people, a number of sittings were required.

Around 5:00 p.m., local guests went home to milk their cows, slop their pigs, and feed the chickens. They did their chores as quickly as possible because they all wanted to get back to the wedding at the Sawatzky farm.

The Evening of the Wedding Day

When the guests arrived back at Sawatzky's, it was *Pulta* (wedding gift) time. The bridal couple opened the wedding gifts they had received from their guests. There were buckets for milking, salt and pepper shakers, bowls, cups, tea towels, and more.

Supper for all the guests followed *Pulta*. On the menu was hot Cabbage *Borscht*, cold *Plüme Mooss* brought up from the cellar, loaves of sliced crusty homemade bread, slices of bologna bought for seven cents a pound at Gallant's store in Letellier, and cold roasted beef.

Again the women and girls washed the dishes and filled the serving bowls for each sitting so that everyone had enough to eat at the Sawatzky wedding. It would be a shame and an embarrassment to run out of food.

After everyone had eaten and all the dishes were done, it was time for the evening festivities. Nettie could finally get into her white wedding dress.

The wedding dance took place in the little house that Nettie's grandma and grandpa Sawatzky had lived in. It was on the Sawatzky yard. The local musicians made up the band. They played polkas, schottisches and square dances. Everyone danced, especially Nettie and her new husband, Peter.

At midnight, more food was served. That meal was known as *Freestikj* (breakfast) and everyone was invited to buns, cold cuts, cheese and pickles. The music

Peter and Nettie on their wedding day in the garden at Johan Sawatzky's home (courtesy of Nettie Neufeld)

went on. Nettie and Peter, and as many guests as the house could hold at once, danced the night away. Nettie went to bed at 4:00 a.m. Her feet were very, very sore. They weren't sore from dancing, but from wearing those new shoes.

The wedding and the marriage were blessed. Nettie and Peter had many wonderful years together, farming, raising their family, and always being there for friends, family and neighbours. The two brought much joy to many people.

Peter has passed away. He is remembered with much love, and Nettie carries on the tradition of making everyone welcome in her home, and visiting with friends, family, and neighbours.

Jakob's Wedding

Johan M. and Helena Sawatzky
|
Tina Heinrich Nettie **Jakob** Helen Mary Marge Anna John Diedrich Willie

Canadian boys were fighting in Europe for the Allies. Helena and Johan's second son Jakob was engaged to be married to Helen Abrams. Jakob and Helen wanted a dance at their wedding to celebrate their marriage vows. It was the custom, but customs changed during the long war years.

During the war years, dances did not follow the exchange of marriage vows as had traditionally been the custom. Johan thought that it was not right for Jakob and Helen to have a wedding dance. *"Nijch wan de Nobasch Junges dart em Kjrijch senn* (Not when the neighbours' boys are there in the war)." Johan explained to his son that it was not right that they should be celebrating when so many young men of Jakob's age were putting down their lives in a faraway land. Those men would never dance with their sweethearts.

Johan was a Mennonite. That meant he was a pacifist and he did not believe in fighting. He grieved for the families in the neighbouring communities of Letellier, Emerson, St. Jean Baptiste, as well as some Mennonite families who all had sons overseas fighting in the European conflict. Johan knew that those families lived from day to day hoping and praying that the telegram saying, "Your son is missing in action" would never come. He worried for the neighbours' boys who were overseas fighting in the cold and wet trenches, fearing for their lives. He could only imagine how hard it must have been for his French Catholic neighbours when they said Bon Voyage to their sons as they saw them off at the train station that ultimately lead to the battlefields. For many, it would be their last Bon Voyage.

Although Johan did not say the words or show his feelings, he was relieved that his own sons were spared from the great battle overseas. Without wanting to do so, Johan made his son Jakob and his bride Helen feel badly for even wanting a dance at their wedding. Wouldn't it have been nice if he could have said to Jakob, "Jakob, my son, I too would like to dance at your wedding, but it would make me feel badly knowing that so many of my friends' sons may never dance at all. If you and Helen don't mind, I would rather celebrate my love for you, and the love that you have for each other, without a dance?" Maybe that is how Johan felt, but did not have the words to say it.

Annie J and Henry D.

Peter S. and Katharina Hildebrand
|
Henry D.

Johan M. and Helena Sawatzky
|
Annie J (Anna)

It was 1943. Annie J was 16. Her real name was Anna, but there were so many Anna's in the one-room school house in Blumenthal, that the teacher made changes to names so that the students knew whom he was calling. Annie J's dark hazel eyes and her wild thick brunette curls made many a local boy's head turn. She would soon be 17. Annie J lived on the farm with her strict father, Johan M., and with her mother and brothers and sisters. Annie J's father was especially strict with her because she was his youngest and his most headstrong daughter. He worried about her because, unlike her five older sisters, Annie J did not necessarily follow his directions just because he said so.

Since Annie J's mother Helena was often not well, her girls, including Annie J, had to do the housework and gardening under Helena's watchful eye. Annie J worked hard, but she was only 16, and she wanted to have some fun.

One warm summer day, at a local wedding attended by many community folks, Annie J noticed a young blonde boy with ice-blue eyes. He looked like he could be about her age, and he was lounging about with some fellows from another district. He certainly was not from Annie J's district of Blumenthal. She knew all the Blumenthal boys, and Annie J had no interest in any of them. This dashing blond with the intense blue eyes was from Edenburg. Everyone in Blumenthal, including Annie J, knew that no good ever came from those Edenburg boys. It was common knowledge that Edenburgers were wild and unruly. Annie J learned that this particular fellow had two older brothers who were overseas fighting in the war.

Annie J had been taught all her life that it was wrong to fight, and that no self-respecting Mennonite boy would enlist in the army. Yes, enlist. It was rumoured the two Edenburg boys had chosen to go overseas. They did not have to go. They had not been conscripted. Many Mennonite boys were conscientious objectors. Her aunts were speculating about those Edenburg boys and gossiping about a family who let their boys go to war. Annie J heard someone call the blond boy, Henry. "What kind of boy was this Henry?" Annie J wondered. Was he like his brothers? Was he like those other wild Edenburgers she had heard about?

Her curiosity about this boy with the wild reputation was more intense than she wanted to admit even to herself. She hoped he was curious about her too.

Henry was indeed interested in the petite, dark-haired beauty with the slight smile. He shyly invited her to join him and his buddy, who was dating Annie J's sister, to go to a movie in Neche, North Dakota, about a forty-five minute drive from the Sawatzky home. Annie J accepted his invitation, thinking that her father probably would

Anna (Annie J) Sawatzky

Henry D. Hildebrand

At the end of the evening, the boys dropped Annie J and her sister off at their farm. The sisters tiptoed into the house, quiet as shadows, avoiding every creaky board on the floor. They did not want to wake up anyone in the house. They had no idea what was waiting for them.

Their father Johan was rocking back and forth in his wooden rocking chair, waiting for his girls to come home. He paid no attention to Annie J's sister. She quietly slithered off to her bed. Johan was waiting for Annie J. His dark, intense face frightened her. The full force of his wrath fell upon her. She had seen her father angry many times before, but never like this. He shouted at his wispy daughter, hurling insults at the boy from Edenburg whose company she had just enjoyed. He berated the family that had raised him. Her father didn't stop there. He questioned the integrity of his very own little girl standing in front of him, insulting her and the boy. Annie J felt as small and insignificant as the infant spider creeping across the shiny living-room linoleum.

When her father had exhausted all his anger, Annie J was left alone without anyone to soothe her battered feelings, or to hold her while her tears washed over her cheeks. Her sisters could not comfort her. They were too afraid of what their father might say to them if he thought they were siding with Annie J. She knew her mother would not be there to give her any solace. Her mother ached for her young daughter, but Annie J would never know that. A good wife never contradicted her husband and for her mother to side with her daughter in this situation would be terribly wrong.

Annie J had enjoyed her evening with that Henry boy from Edenburg so much that she thought she would like to see him again despite her father's dire warnings and threats. She did see him again and again, no matter how vehemently her father objected. Eventually he gave up opposing the courtship of the two young sweethearts. He knew he wouldn't and couldn't change his girl's mind about that boy. Goodness knows, he had tried. He had seen the signs of love in his other daughters, and when those signs were there, there was no changing a girl's mind.

On September 21, 1947 the two young people were married. Johan M. and his son-in-law slowly developed a mutual respect, and by the time Johan M. died in the fall of 1960, the two men were able to share a chuckle together.

Smiles and Chuckles

Some times were tough, and some times were funny.

Peter S. Hildebrand frequently reminded his children, "It's time to get up. All the neighbours are working in the fields." When evening came, his children used his strategy with, "Time to quit working. All the neighbours have gone home." Peter S. replied to his children, "Oh, we don't model ourselves after our neighbours."

"*Junges, stot opp* (Boys, get up), the day after tomorrow is mid week, and we have not yet done any work," was Peter S. Hildebrand's wake up call to his sons on Monday mornings.

Balloons

Peter S. and **Katharina** Hildebrand

|

Katharina Maria Helen **Olga** Anna Peter Abram (Alan) Henrietta Henry Eva

The two barefooted little sisters were meandering down the dusty dirt road with the grass growing in the middle where the wheels of cars and buggies rarely touched. The girls were chattering about the good time they had just had with their cousins where they had played all afternoon. The cousins lived a half mile down the dusty dirt road from their farmhouse.

The girls shuffled along, kicking pebbles and creating little clouds of dust with their dirty feet. They wandered from one side of the road to the other like they were snakes. As was their habit, they kept their eyes on the road and ditches, looking for treasures. Once, they had found a discarded package of cigarettes that had a whole cigarette in it. Another time they had found an old King George coin. The only reason they found the coin was because a horse hoof had kicked it up from a clump of mud. This day, they were looking from force of habit. Out of nowhere came a glint. The setting sun was reflected from something on the ground. There was something shiny at the edge of the grass growing in the middle of the road. Could it be a whole quarter? That would be a lot of money. It could buy at least two ice-cream cones and maybe a soda or two.

It wasn't a quarter. It was a little round tin box. They struggled to open it. When they finally jarred it open; they found—of all things to store in a tin box—balloons! The balloons were wrapped in shiny silver paper. What a wonderful surprise. The girls ran home the rest of the way to show their mother Katharina their newly discovered treasure. They blew up the balloons and released them to fly about as the air escaped from them, making a "pork-and-beans" sound. They blew up the balloons again, released them, and let them zoom around the kitchen like drunken flies. The children laughed and giggled as they chased the funny balloons.

Katharina thought that it was a somewhat unusual presentation of balloons—wrapped in silver paper and stored in a shiny tin box. She consulted with her sister-in-law, Gertrude, who lived the half mile down the dusty dirt road.

"*Trütji* (Gertrude)," she said, "*waut senn de Dinga— de Loftblose daut de Kjinga met späle? De senn werkjlijch sposijch* (What are those things—those balloons the children are playing with? They sure are funny)."

Gertrude's only response was, "*Komm häa* (Come here)." She beckoned Katharina to a corner, well out of earshot of the children's long eavesdropping ears. Gertrude whispered something into Katharina's ears. Katharina's face and ears and neck turned as red as the beets in the pickle jar. She bustled over to the balloon-bouncing children, grabbed the offending baubles, and threw them into the cookstove. The children were dumbstruck. What was their mother thinking? She was destroying their newest, most favourite toys. She was discarding toys that weren't broken. The balloons still had plenty of play left in them. Katharina neither explained nor apologized—she only told the children they had chores to do and they'd best get at them real soon.

Blackmail

Peter S. and Katharina Hildebrand
|
Henry

Jacob and Gertrude Hildebrand
|
Peter

Little Henry and little Peter were nine years old and they were the best of friends. The two boys did as much together as their parents would permit. When they had to feed the pigs and the chickens, milk the cows, or feed the horses their rations of oats, they did it together. First they went to Peter's farm to do the chores, and then they went to Henry's farm to do the chores. It did not matter to the two little fellows that they lived half-a-mile apart. At such an early age they already understood that sharing a load was halving the load. They also knew that when they worked together, it was not really work. It was fun.

The boys played together during school recess, after school, and during summer holidays, and then they were together at their Grandma and Grandpa Hildebrand's family gatherings because their fathers were brothers. That meant they had the same Hildebrand grandparents. These family gatherings happened regularly in Mennonite homes—Christmas, Good Friday, Easter, Pentecost, Ascension Day and on many Sundays.

In the summer time, the boys spent hour after hour catching gophers. Selling gopher tails to the municipality was their only source of revenue. They idled away the season by playing ball and skinny-dipping in the pond that had two hills on each side like the bumps under their older sisters' sweaters.

As the summer days grew longer, the sun turned their hair to a pale yellow and darkened their freckles. The boys grew like the milkweed in the ditch. By summer's end, their ankles were showing between the bottom of their pant legs and the tops of their work shoes—that is, on the days they were wearing shoes instead of running about in bare feet.

In the wintertime, they skated, played hockey on the frozen pond, built snow houses with rooms, and on occasion, got into a little mischief. Both boys had younger and older brothers and sisters who were wonderful targets for teasing and tricking. They tricked more than just their brothers and

– This story was told to the author by her father's cousin Peter Hildebrand.

---

sisters though.

By chance, Peter had learned about where babies came from. He had been told all the details from the first kiss to the last sigh, and he was eager to tell his cousin Henry everything he had learned.

At the first opportunity when the two youngsters were feeding the sow that was nursing her piglets at Peter's farm, Peter told Henry the whole story about where babies came from, in graphic detail. Peter left nothing out. Absolutely nothing.

Henry was shocked. He knew that his very own parents had had ten children by that time, and he knew they would never ever do that. His only response to Peter was "*Nijch Mutt en Pau* (Not Mom and Dad)." Peter assured him that, yes, Henry's "*Mutt en Pau*" had indeed done just that.

Little Henry would not and could not believe Peter's story. Babies were delivered by storks, and that was that. Peter was not telling him the truth.

His mother and father would never do that. Not even once. How could Peter even think of such things? He knew Peter was lying and this was not funny. Henry, however, was never one to let an opportunity go by.

In the next months, Peter and Henry learned the meaning of the word "blackmail". Henry only needed to say to Peter "I'll tell your Mama if you don't...", and Peter knew exactly what Henry meant. If Peter did not do as Henry wished, Henry would tell Peter's mother of the horrible lie that Peter had told him about where babies came from. Peter was Henry's very own hired-hand for the season, and Henry milked it for all it was worth.

Over time, the two boys came to believe Peter's "lie". Both Henry and Peter became fathers of five children each. If Peter had called Henry's bluff, would Henry have had the courage to repeat Peter's story to Peter's mother?

Sparrows Anyone?

Peter S. and Katharina Hildebrand
|
Katharina Maria Helen Olga Anna Peter Abram Henrietta **Henry** Eva

One fall evening in the mid 1930s, young Henry went to visit the Wall family with his mother and father, Peter and Katharina Hildebrand. The Walls lived three miles away from the Hildebrands. Their son Armin was Henry's good friend. The two boys knew each other because their schools competed against each other in baseball games—Edenthal (Armin's team) versus Edenburg (Henry's team).

As soon as Henry arrived at Armin's home, the two boys began to plot their evening. Their plans did not include George, Armin's naïve little eight-year-old brother. George could play by himself and leave them be. As far as they were concerned, George could do anything he wanted, as long as he left them alone.

The Walls had a brand new flashlight. In those days a flashlight was a useful novelty and it was not to be played with. It was to be used sparingly and only when absolutely necessary. *"Daut es nijch en späl Dinkj* (It is not a toy)," were Mrs. Wall's words to her boys. George and Armin would have loved to use the flashlight and pretend that they were sending SOS signals from a sinking ship, or that they were giant fireflies blinking in the night.

Henry and Armin threw caution to the wind. They took the flashlight from its storage place and dashed out to the barn. Their destination was the big hayloft filled with mountains of warm-smelling hay. In the hayloft, Armin turned on the flashlight. The boys knew they had to be very careful with it because it had to go back exactly where it had come from, looking like it had never moved a millimeter from its storage place. The flashlight cast a funnel of light into the corners of the loft, and up into the rafters. The boys were looking for something and it did not take long before the cone of light pointed to what they were looking for. There, perched on the rafters, just as they had suspected, were rows of sparrows, lined up like clothespins on the outside clothes line. The birds were cuddling like lovers. The sparrows did not move in the glare of the light.

– Story told to the author by George Wall over coffee at the Sheraton Hotel in Winnipeg, August 2, 2000.

They seemed to be hypnotized and glued to the rafters. Henry and Armin approached the birds —closer and closer. The birds did not move. The boys picked the paralyzed sparrows off the rafters like ripe apples from the tree in the backyard. They had plans for the little birds.

Henry and Armin had watched their mothers prepare chickens for the roasting pan lots of times. Surely preparing sparrows for the roaster would be the same, only in miniature. Armin and Henry took the sparrows —three, four, five, in number and chopped off their heads with the hatchet Mr. Wall kept in the barn to chop ice in the wintertime. They released the headless sparrows from their grip to see if they would jump around like chickens with their heads cut off. Then they plucked all the feathers off the tiny birds. The boys pulled out their handy little jack knives that were always in their pockets, and eviscerated the sparrows exactly like their mothers eviscerated chickens.

They gingerly cut across the bottom of each tiny bird, from one baby finger-sized drumstick to the other. Then they inserted their biggish and clumsy adolescent fingers into the cut to pull the tiny wormlike intestines out of the naked birds. They lined the little birds in a row, ready for the oven.

If this was to be a gourmet dish, they would have to cook the tiny fowl. Stealthily they returned to Mrs. Wall's pristine kitchen where everything was sparkling clean and in its place. They quickly put the flashlight back in its rightful place, checking the whereabouts of the parents. Thankfully they were all in the "*Grooti Stow*" (living room) immersed in big-people talk.

The boys found Mrs. Wall's everyday frying pan, put a dollop of homemade butter into it, and set it on the old cook stove. They gently placed each little bird into the pan and watched. The sizzling butter browned the birds to perfection.

Henry and Armin served the miniscule fowl snack in Mrs. Wall's china and offered it to Armin's little brother George who had been keeping his distance from the two adolescents. George was delighted to be a part of the big boys' fun and he was eager to do whatever they wanted, just so that he could be with them. He was honoured to sample the food they had cooked. George trusted the big boys. When they offered them their culinary delight, they tempted George with "*Daut schmakjt sea scheen* (That tastes very good)," even though neither one of them had had the courage to take a bite.

Armin and Henry watched little George in anticipation. Would he really eat the bird meat? George took a bird-sized bite of sparrow. It was very tough. He chewed and chewed. His little nose screwed up as he mustered up the courage to swallow the chunk of meat that his teeth could not break down. He swallowed. With big tear filled eyes, he looked at the big boys, and retorted, "*Dit schmackt oba sea shlajcht* (This tastes awful)."

Henry and Armin howled. George had eaten sparrow and they would never, ever let him forget it. George learned never to trust those big boys in the kitchen again.

Of Legal Age

Peter S. and Katharina Hildebrand
|
Katharina Maria Olga Helen Anna **Peter Abram (Alan)** Henrietta **Henry** Eva

For six years, Henry played ball in the States-Dominion baseball league. The games were played in Manitoba and North Dakota towns. Henry's brothers Alan and Peter were on the same team with him, and Alan was an exceptional player. Regular spectators believed he was good enough to play in the big league.

It was a young league and the team members played for the love of the game. Some of the fellows who had gone overseas to fight in the conflict between 1939 and 1945 were a bit older, but when they returned home, they got right back in the game. Henry's brother Peter was one of those fellows. It was 1945, and the boys had just played a game in Emerson, Manitoba. Their post-game ritual was to have a beer with their competition and the umpire. It did not matter whether the umpire had called them "safe" or "out". What mattered was his love of the game. The umpire was Archie Batchelor. Not only was Archie the umpire, but he was also the regional Royal Canadian Mounted Police officer who served with the Gretna detachment from 1937 to 1947.

While the boys were reliving the game over their beer, Archie struck up a conversation with Peter. Archie commented to Peter on how good the team was and how young the players were. "Yes," said Peter conversationally, forgetting that he was back in civilian life and the boys had to be 21 to drink, "and only two of the fellows are over 21." No sooner had those words passed Peter's lips, when the 18 ball players, with beer in hand, were instantly silenced. The legal drinking age was 21, and every boy knew that Archie was a Royal Canadian Mounted Police. Archie never missed a beat; he carried on with his conversation with Peter. For the moment, he was only an umpire. Lady Luck was on the side of the under 21-year-olds—luckily for Peter.

– This story was told to the author by her father, Henry D. Hildebrand on October 30, 2001.

Willie's Moustaches

Johan M. and Helena Sawatzky

|

Tina Nettie Heinrich Jakob Helen Mary Marge Anna John Diedrich **Willie**

Willie was a curious little fellow. During the days and months before he learned to walk, he crawled all over the waxed linoleum floors that his older sisters kept spotless and shiny as a new penny. Willie also crawled all over the yard that his sisters could not possibly keep clean. It was difficult enough to keep the house clean, never mind trying to pick up after the chickens that left their droppings on the farmyard. Willie crawled about the house and yard to learn everything about his world. He explored by touching, smelling, listening, and tasting. His eyes were level with his little body on all four limbs—about eighteen inches above ground level. Through those eyes, he observed his miniscule world while his pursed lips kept his swollen rubber soother firmly locked in his mouth.

When he was outdoors on his family farm in Blumenthal, he was not alone. Willie's pretty older sisters were always bustling about, hoeing the garden, baking, or hanging the laundry way up high on the clothesline. From his four-point crawling position, Willie could not even reach his father's droopy long johns hanging from the line. They were too high for him to tug. While his sisters did the heavy housework, Willie's mother sat under a shade tree taking the ends off freshly picked green beans for that savoury *Jreene Schauble Sup* (Green Bean Soup) that Willie loved. He knew that *Jreene Schauble Sup* was especially delicious when his mother poured fresh cream into his bowl of soup. He liked the soup best with crusty buns that had just come out of the oven.

Willie and his slightly older brother Diedrich played in the dirt close to their mother. Nearby their father was repairing machinery for the upcoming harvest. Besides all the family members surrounding Willie, the chickens also roamed freely about the yard, dropping the occasional feather and chalky wormlike manure.

Little Willie crawled over everything in his way. His short legs and arms carried him all over the yard and the soother in his mouth was like a radar beam, pointing him in the direction that

Sketch by Katie Altendorf Cable © 2003

– This story was told at the Sawatzky family gathering on July 14, 2001. On January 11, 2002, Nettie Neufeld, the author's aunt, told the story in more detail.

he was headed. He crawled over small stones left from the gravel that had been worked into the driveway; over chicken droppings; and over clumps of grass that had escaped the jaws of the grazing cows. Willie paused for only one thing. He paused for the feathers that the chickens had lost during their foraging and pecking. Willie picked up each feather, held it between his pudgy thumb and forefinger, and examined it closely. Then he carefully placed it under his nose behind his soother. The soother gripped the feather and kept it in its place between Willie's nose and mouth. As the day progressed, Willie parked one feather after another behind his soother, giving him the appearance of a moustached infant.

One day his moustache would be lopsided and droopy. Another day it would be small and fluffy. His moustache of the day depended on his feather finds. He had the opportunity to create a great variety of different moustaches in a day because he got a "shave" each time he took his soother out of his mouth to have a sip of water or eat a snack. Whenever the soother had to come out of Willie's mouth, a feather shower fell from his mouth to the ground. Little Willie wasted no time growing a new moustache. As long as there were chickens roaming about the yard, little Willie would not remain clean-shaven for long.

Little Diedrich's Soother

Johan M. and Helena Sawatzky

|

Tina Nettie Heinrich Jakob Helen Mary Marge Anna John **Diedrich** Willie

---

Little Diedrich loved his soother. The brownish, rubbery bulb felt just perfect in his mouth when he sucked it. All his worries went far away from him every time he popped his soother into his mouth. It was so comforting. Diedrich especially liked to have his soother when he took his afternoon nap and when he went to bed at night. It also felt very nice in his mouth when he and his baby brother Willie were playing on the floor with their tractors.

The day came when Diedrich's Mama and Papa thought Diedrich was old enough to set aside his baby things and it was time to start the business of growing up. The first step was for Diedrich to give up his soother. In their opinion, he did not need it anymore. Diedrich disagreed. He loved his soother. His Mama and Papa took his soother away. It was cruel of them to do that to their Diedrich.

Diedrich complained, whined, and begged. He wanted his Mama and Papa to give him back his soother, but they did not listen to him. Diedrich was desperate. Even though he was very young, he understood when his Mama and Papa had put their respective feet down. He could not change their minds.

Diedrich pondered over his problem. He eventually came up with a solution. He remembered that his little friend Susie Neufeld, who lived with her Mama and Papa just east of where Diedrich lived, had a soother exactly like his. Susie's soother was just as bulbous and soft as the one that his Mama and Papa had stolen from him.

Diedrich headed east to Susie's home. His short legs and determination took him through the grain fields that were as tall as a forest to the pint-sized Diedrich. They took him through the ditches filled

– Story told to the author by her Uncle Dick (Little Diedrich) at the July 14, 2001 Sawatzky family reunion.

with prickly weeds that brushed his shoulders and over the dusty country road with the grooves from horses' hooves and tire tracks. When he finally arrived at Susie's home, he went directly to find Susie. She and her sister were playing with their rag dolls, and much to Diedrich's delight, Susie had her soother in her mouth, precisely where he had hoped it would be. Diedrich marched over to Susie and plucked the soother from her mouth. He popped the warm, wet, rubbery blob into his mouth and felt the comfort that the soother gave him wash over his entire little being. Without a thank you or a wave, he turned around and walked straight back home, his face beaming like the face of a baby angel. Life was good.

Diedrich's Dilemma

Johan M. and Helena Sawatzky
|
Tina Nettie Heinrich Jakob Helena Mary Marge Anna John **Diedrich** Willie

Diedrich was just a little fellow. When his father needed to take his car for business or pleasure, Diedrich usually went along with him. When they got home, Diedrich always hopped out of the car and carried on with his playing or followed his father around the yard.

One day, when Diedrich had gone out with his father in the family car, he was quietly playing in the back seat while driving back home. Soon he got very sleepy and fell asleep, as children do.

Diedrich and his father got home. His father parked the car in the garage that was 200 metres south of the house. He locked the garage door, and went into the house. He did not give Diedrich a thought. He assumed his little curly haired son had jumped out of the car way ahead of him.

The next day Johan had to go out on the road early in the morning. When he opened the wooden garage door, there was his little boy, crying his heart out. Diedrich's eyes were red and puffy from weeping and his face was stained from the many tears. Johan was surprised to see his distressed young son up so early, and asked him, "*Jung, waut west dü nü aul op* (Boy, why are you up so early)?"

It never occurred to him that Diedrich had had a sleep-over in the garage. Diedrich was not pleased. At the very least his father should have missed him.

Stroo Enne Beksi
(Straw in the Pants)

Johan M. and Helena Sawatzky

|

Tina **Nettie** Heinrich Jacob Helen Mary Marge Anna John **Diedrich** Willie

Diedrich believed that the sun rose and set on him. He was a normal baby. He had skills, needs, and desires that any mother would accept as stages of normal child development. Since he was the youngest in the family for at least a little while, he was that very special baby, the prince. That honourable role was his until little baby Willie arrived on the scene.

Diedrich was of the opinion that all his older sisters, five in number, were there to wait upon his every beck and call. They desperately wanted him to be toilet trained, but he did not share their urgency. He also did not feel guilt or remorse about presenting them with dirty diapers—piles of dirty diapers.

His sister Nettie was getting more than just a little impatient with this little guy who thought he could soil his diapers without feeling any sense of obligation to use the outhouse with the two holes in it. If he had used the outhouse, he could have sat in comfort, left the door open for air exchange, and saved himself from the unpleasantness of a stinky, sticky bottom. Despite this opportunity for independence, Diedrich chose to soil his diapers and to have his sister Nettie change them for him.

Nettie found no pleasure in dealing with Diedrich's poopy diapers. She made it her mission to get Diedrich to want to be toilet trained. Nettie was a *Kjinjafrind* (children's friend) and she was respectful of her little brother's wishes. She kneeled down in front of the little boy so that she was at his eye level. She looked him in the eye, and sweetly said to him, "*Diedrich, du kaust wäle* (Diedrich, you can choose). *Dü kaust gaunss auleen no de Tsekjreet gone* (You can go to the outhouse all by yourself), *ooda ejk woa die Stroo enne Bekjsi* (or I'll put straw into your pants)."

Diedrich thought his sister was joking. He laughed at her joke. His sister was so funny. Diedrich did not go to the outhouse all by himself. Nettie understood that to mean that Diedrich had chosen to have *Stroo enne Bekjsi*. She would honour his choice. She carefully lined his pants with the pretty, yellow, prickly straw from the dusty hayloft.

Diedrich could hardly believe that his loving sister who had always changed his diapers and washed his bottom with fresh clean water, had actually done this to him. Surely, she had not really meant those words about going to the outhouse all by himself, and the business about *Stroo enne Bekjsi*. Nettie would never do that to him. Nettie loved him. Nonetheless, Diedrich was feeling the itchy, scratchy straw rub against his smooth bottom. It felt awful. Every time he moved, the straw scratched parts that had only ever been touched by nice soft white diapers. No matter how little Diedrich pleaded with Nettie, she did not remove the straw until he used the outhouse. She reminded him what a big boy he was. She told him that she knew he would do the right thing. Soon he chose to use the outhouse all by himself. Anything was better than *Stroo enne Bekjsi*.

Red Hot Peppers

Johan M. and Helena Sawatzky
|
Tina Nettie Heinrich Jakob Helena Mary Marge Anna **John Diedrich** Willie

Diedrich and John loved to visit their Sawatzky grandparents. Their grandma and grandpa had moved from their little house in Blumenthal to their new place in the town of Altona. Their grandparents had a house, a barn, a horse, and a small vegetable garden that grew the usual Manitoba-Mennnonite variety of vegetables and herbs.

Some things were the same in town as they were at home. Their grandparents' garden had the same things that their garden in Blumenthal had. There were rows of carrots, beans, potatoes, kohlrabi, red beets, juicy red tomatoes, green pea pods, and herbs to flavour soups. There was woody summer savoury to give green bean soup its own distinctive flavour; there was lush green parsley to flavour butter soup made of noodles, potatoes, and butter; and there was tall, lanky dill with its pale green seeded crown scattered about the garden. The dill was an essential ingredient for cooking Cabbage *Borscht*.

Even though some things were the same, the two little boys loved to visit their grandparents because other things were so different in town from the way they were at home on their farm. The lads explored the yard, looking for things that were new and unusual. On the farm they had big pigs, cows, and horses. Their grandpa only had one horse. Their own garden in Blumenthal was huge compared to their grandparents' baby-sized garden. In town, the houses were really close together. On the farm, the neighbours' houses were wheat fields apart.

On one visit to their grandparents' home, John and Diedrich explored their grandparents' garden, commenting on how short the rows were and how close together they were. They carefully took giant-high steps over the rows of plants with the ripened fruit, just as they had been taught to do. Everything was familiar to them until they came upon that one row of something that was unusual, but looked delicious. They had never seen that plant in their garden in Blumenthal. What was that strange fruit?

The plant was dark green. It was nothing like a

tomato plant, yet it had red fruit. It looked a little like a bean plant, but the boys had only seen green beans and yellow beans—never red beans.

They knew that red tomatoes tasted very good, even though they could be messy. Sometimes when they ate tomatoes, they dribbled the juice on their clothes. They were wearing their Sunday clothes and their mother would not be pleased with her little boys if they ate that lovely red fruit, and it dribbled down their clean crisp shirts. They would be careful they told themselves. They knew that everything in the garden, except the hot onions, tasted good. Some of the vegetables tasted better when their mother cooked them, but it was fun to eat things raw right out of the garden.

The boys could not resist the red fruit. They were tempted just as Adam had been tempted by the apple. They carefully picked one dark-red fruit from the plant. It felt cool and it was smooth like an apple.

They examined every angle carefully, sniffed it, and took a bite. Diedrich took the first bite. Oh no, what was it? Something was burning his mouth. Little Diedrich could not stop the burn. He cried and rubbed away his tears. Now his eyes burned too. Diedrich had bitten into a nasty red-hot pepper. What a horrible thing it was. How did something so pretty, yet so nasty, get into their grandparents' garden? Their own mother never grew anything in her garden that hurt children. Was this a trick?

The boys ran indoors to alert all the adults that something horrible was growing in the garden. They expected sympathy. Surely all the big people would feel sorry for them. There was no sympathy, not even when Diedrich's eyes puffed up so much that he could hardly see. The big people only laughed at the little boys.

Diedrich and John did not think that was very nice. They comforted each other as they heard their grandfather tell the big people about a seed he had brought from Mexico and planted in the garden. He called it *Jalopeña*.

Bunny Business

Johan M. and Helena Sawatzky
|
Tina Nettie Heinrich Jakob Helen Mary Marge Anna John **Diedrich** Willie

Summer after summer, little Diedrich spent his days with his *Auntji Mum* (Aunt Anne) and *Oom Kjnaltz* (Uncle Cornelius). They lived in the village of Sommerfeld, which was only a few miles west of where Diedrich lived with his mother, his father, and his brothers and sisters. In his aunt's eyes, little Diedrich could do no wrong. Diedrich loved that. When he was with his aunt, he knew that he was special. She only had two children who needed her attention. Diedrich's mother had many children, so he did not get nearly as much attention from his mother as he thought he deserved.

If his *Auntji Mum's* children Jake or Tina ever had a little spat with Diedrich or even looked at him with unfriendly eyes, Diedrich's aunt would rush to his defense and scold her own children. They should always be nice to their little cousin Diedrich.

One summer when Diedrich stayed with his aunt and uncle, their son Jake was in the business of raising rabbits. Jake planned to sell the rabbits in the fall for a handsome price. Jake was older and bigger than Diedrich, and so when he gave Diedrich an order, Diedrich listened. Jake instructed Diedrich to watch a pair of rabbits very closely. Jake told Diedrich that he should not let his eyes look away from the rabbits—not even for a second. Diedrich's job was to catch the rabbits mating, and as soon as that happened, he was to report the incident to Jake. Once the rabbits had mated, Jake intended to separate the pair to keep them from harming each other. Jake had learned that after rabbits mated, they sometimes seriously injured each other. Jake did not want that to happen. He wanted the rabbits to keep on mating and provide him with many bunnies to sell. For Jake, this was potentially a sustainable business.

– Story told to the author by her Uncle Dick, (Diedrich) May 10, 2002.

Diedrich took his job very seriously. He watched the two rabbits day in and day out. This was a very hard job for a little boy who wanted to play with his toys or follow his *Oom Kjnaltz* around the farmyard. It did not take long before Diedrich got tired and weary of his job. He wanted to quit, but he had not yet seen the rabbits mate. He made an executive decision. He did not know what an executive decision was, but he made a decision without consulting Jake. He decided to tell Jake a little lie. Diedrich boldly approached his big cousin and announced that he had seen the rabbits mate. Jake immediately put the rabbits into separate cages and waited for the arrival of little bunnies. Jake waited and he waited. No bunnies arrived. Jake was puzzled. How could that be? He knew that after rabbits mated, it did not take long before baby bunnies appeared. Why was this time different? Jake got suspicious of his little cousin Diedrich. Had he really seen the rabbits mate? What, in fact, had he seen? When Jake asked Diedrich those difficult questions, Diedrich caved under the pressure of the inquisition. He looked down at his dusty shoes, and quietly said to his cousin. "*Daut wea nijch soo. Ejk sach daut goanijch* (It was not true. I did not see that at all)."

Jake wanted to show his bratty little cousin the back of his hand, but he did not dare because he knew how his parents thought the sun rose and set on their little nephew. Jake was very disappointed. There would be no bunnies to sell in fall. Jake's pockets would be flat and not bulging from the bunny profits that he had already seen in his mind. Jake never asked Diedrich to watch his rabbits again!

Go West Young Men

Peter S. and Katharina Hildebrand
|
Tina Maria Helen Olga Anna Peter Abram Henrietta **Henry** Eva

---

Four young Mennonite lads, Henry, Ed, Benno, and John were heading west and leaving their southern Manitoba farm homes for the first time. The young men, in their early twenties, were heading west to British Columbia in Benno's 1929 Model A Ford. It was the autumn of 1947.

The four young men had made it all the way to the foothills of the Teton mountain range in Montana in Benno's Model A. It could barely climb to a speed of 25 miles per hour. Ed's stray foot had smashed the rear window in the midst of a back-seat wrestling match, and eighteen years of gravel-and-dirt road driving had left the vehicle looking mighty tired and weary. In Montana, the car came to a grinding halt. The young men piled out of the car. They lifted the hood that opened from the side to see what was wrong. It did not take them long to diagnose the problem.

There was a short in the distributor. The fellows knew that they were far from a service station, but all four of them were resourceful farmers and they knew how to solve mechanical problems. Unfortunately, they had none of the right tools or parts with them to repair the car. It wasn't long before young Ed came up with a solution. At the least, he could solve the problem temporarily. He proudly proclaimed to his buddies, "*Ekj weit woo wie daut kjenne trajcht moake* (I know how we can fix it)." He smirked at his buddies and slowly slipped his hand into the pocket of his baggy drapes.

He pulled out a shiny package and flashed it in front of his friends like a magician pulling a rabbit out of a hat. They all recognized the package, but were too embarrassed to comment on Ed's "solution". They snickered, just to be cool, but none of them could understand why Ed was pulling the little silver package out of his pocket at such a time. First of all, there were no girls around, and secondly, they did not have time for his shenanigans. They had to get the car repaired if they wanted to get to British Columbia before the Montana snows kept them from moving forward. This was no time for Ed's pranks. With the flair of

Ed, John, Benno and the 1929 Model A Ford (courtesy of Henry D. Hildebrand)

Henry D. Hildebrand took the photograph of his friend Benno, John Schroeder his brother-in-law, and his cousin Ed Hildebrand, on their journey through Montana on their way to British Columbia for a vacation, and possibly employment.

– Story told by Henry D. Hildebrand to his daughter, the author, on September 2, 2002 after his wife's birthday party at the author's home.

a magician, Ed opened the shiny package, took out the rubbery balloon inside, and slipped it over the distributor cap.

The boys piled back into the car. Benno crossed his fingers for good luck and turned the key to the ignition of the Model A. To everyone's relief, the Model A sputtered and started. They were eager to get to the nearest service station in Billings, Montana before their "solution" broke down. Not one of the boys was confident that Ed's remedy would last for long. When they got to Billings, they drove into the biggest service station lot that the boys had ever seen. It had a bay for every part of a car's body—brakes, mufflers, shocks, tires, and the list went on. The four Manitoba boys had only ever seen garages with single bays that serviced one car at a time.

The boys explained their situation to the mechanic who opened the hood from the side to take a close look at the distributor cap problem. The mechanic could not believe what he saw. With the precision of a brain surgeon, using a pair of needle-nosed pliers; the mechanic removed the rubber "safety valve". He held it up high for everyone in the garage to see. His astonishment quickly turned into roars of laughter. He showed it to the muffler man who broke out in giant guffaws. He showed it to the radiator man who held his sides because he was laughing so hard and he showed it to the tire man who almost choked on his coffee. In no time, everyone in the whole garage was laughing, including the retired schoolteacher who had just brought her car in for an oil change.

Once he could work without breaking into howls of laughter, the mechanic got down to business. He fixed the car for the boys. He would not let the boys give him one thin dime for his work. He said they had already paid him. The knee-slapping laughter that the four Mennonite lads from Manitoba had brought to the service station was worth a whole lot more than they would ever charge.

Wolf Whistles

– Told to the author by her father, Henry D. Hildebrand (one of the four lads), on September 2, 2002.

The four Manitoban lads Ed, Henry Benno, and John were continuing on their way to British Columbia after they had Benno's 1929 Model A Ford repaired in Billings, Montana. They had never been in Billings before, so they thought they might take a little spin around town to see the sights.

Their first sighting of interest was a pair of young lovers walking down the street, hand in hand. The boys thought that the young lady was very easy to look at, and they had no hesitations acknowledging that. All four of them turned their heads in unison to admire the young lady and wolf whistle at her. Wolf whistling was not politically incorrect in 1947. Nonetheless, the young lady's companion took mighty exception to the behaviour of the four young Manitoban boys. He dropped his lady's hand and ran after the cheeky four lads in the Model A, shouting at them and admonishing them for their rude behaviour. Fortunately for the four lads, their vehicle could drive at the speed of 25 miles per hour, and the raging jealous lover could not run quite that fast.

The Horse on the Box

Johan M. and Helena Sawatzky
|
Tina Nettie Heinrich Jakob Helen Mary Marge Anna John Diedrich Willie

It was the early 1950s. Johan was way ahead of the times. Long before Pierre Elliot Trudeau proclaimed Canada to be a bilingual country, Johan was doing his personal best to promote positive multicultural and bilingual relationships.

Johan and Helena's farm was adjacent to the Parent family farm. Johan spoke no French; Mr. Parent spoke no *Plautdietsch* (Low German); and both men spoke a few words of English. Mr. Parent spoke English with a thick French accent and Johan spoke English with a flat *Plautdietsch* accent. The two men never let the language differences come between their friendship. They were good neighbours to each other.

As youngsters, the Sawatzky children and the Parent children played baseball together. Although the Parent children spoke French at home and the Sawatzky children spoke *Plautdietsch* at home, the children communicated easily because they had all learned English in school. Besides, when Anna Sawatzky and Norbert Parent played ball with their brothers and sisters, they all knew baseball language. Each child knew what "strike three" and "safe on first" meant.

When Johan and Mr. Parent had a conversation, they communicated with their hands and a few English words mixed in with their respective mother tongues. They understood each other—laughing, pointing, and nodding in agreement.

Both men were farmers. They raised livestock for their meat and they grew oats, wheat, barley, and sugar beets. During the sugar-beet harvest, Johan and his neighbours delivered their beets to the beet dump at Christie Siding.

While the farmers waited to unload their truckloads of sugar beets at the dump, there was always plenty of time for the farmers to visit with each other. The line-up of loaded beet trucks waiting to dump their beets was very long and slow during the height of the harvest season. One year just before beet harvesting season Johan had purchased a new dark blue one-ton Mercury truck with a hoist. Like the other farmers, he enjoyed discussing the qualities of machinery and the finer points of each little bell-and-whistle on the equipment.

Johan walked along the long line-up of beet trucks waiting to dump their load of beets to be transported to Winnipeg by train. In Winnipeg the beets were refined into sugar at a big factory. The farmers waiting in their trucks welcomed a conversation with Johan. It staved off the boredom of waiting.

Along his walk, Johan struck up a conversation with Mr. Dansereau. Like Mr. Parent, Mr. Dansereau mixed in a few English words with his French. Johan mixed in a bit of English with his *Plautdietsch*. The two men discussed Johan's new truck, using a few words and a lot of hand signaling. Johan explained the wonderful hoist on his new truck. His mouth could not quite master the "ois" sound in the word "hoist", so he said to Mr. Dansereau, "It is so *händig* (handy) with the horse on the box." Mr. Dansereau knew exactly what Johan meant.

Party Line

Johan M. and **Helena** Sawatzky

|

Tina Nettie Heinrich Jakob Helen Mary Marge Anna John Diedrich Willie

Long before the Manitoba Telephone System provided Manitobans with touch dial, message managers, and cellular telephones, Helena and Johan M. Sawatzky were on a party line. The party line was one telephone line that had numerous household telephone lines connected to it. Whenever someone on the party line was telephoned, all the other people on the line could hear the ring in their own households. Each household on the party line had its own ring. Jake Fehr's ring was two long rings and one short ring. Peter Friesen's ring was three short rings. When anyone on the party line was on the telephone, no one else could use it. However, if one picked up the receiver when someone was having a chat on the telephone, the conversation could be listened to by the person picking up the receiver. Only one phone call could be made on a party line at a time.

If anyone, including Helena, picked up the receiver to make a call, and a neighbour was on the phone, the polite thing to do was to quietly hang up the phone immediately. The person should then wait a respectable amount of time (perhaps 10 or 15 minutes) before lifting the receiver to try to use the phone again. Hopefully by then the neighbour's phone call would have come to an end.

Every household knew the rule: never, ever eavesdrop. The neighbour's telephone conversation was private, and no one else's business. To break that rule was a complete breach of etiquette.

Yet, sometimes Helena's curiosity got the better of her. Sometimes she simply had to *schnack opp* (eavesdrop) on the neighbours' telephone conversations. How else would she know the latest news in the community? Later on in the day, she would report the "news" to her family. She reported that Mrs. Abe Doerksen's forty quarts of dill pickles had spoiled and that Guenther's boy had trapped thirty-seven gophers in one day. Helena had bits and pieces of the details because she only heard parts of conversations. After all, it would have been just too rude and too obvious if she had picked up the receiver as soon as she heard the phone ring for her neighbour.

Later, when the whole story circulated around the district by word of mouth, everyone learned that Mrs. Doerksen only hoped her dill pickles wouldn't spoil and Guenther's boy had caught thirty-seven gophers that one summer. When asked what her source of information was, Helena smiled sheepishly and admitted to her little breach of telephone manners.

Schnacking opp was irresistible when the community was anticipating news of births, illnesses, near deaths, and marriage plans. It was also of great interest to learn about courtships and who got the *Kjiep* (who was told to hit the road in affairs of the heart) the previous Sunday night. How else would anyone ever know how many bushels Ben Friesen got per acre of oats or how many yards of white satin Margaret Unger used to sew her rather generously proportioned daughter's wedding dress?

Mrs. Dueck at the other end of Blumenthal took it upon herself to butt in on conversations when she was *schnacking opp*. She felt compelled to make corrections if what she overheard was not quite accurate

Even though everyone knew that they should not listen in on other peoples' telephone conversations, it was common practice to *schnack opp*—especially when the phone rang at odd hours and when news breaking events were anticipated in the community. Such was the case when the phone rang two long and one short ring at 2:30 in the morning. Two long and one short was Jake Fehr's ring, and Jake's wife looked as though she could be carrying triplets in her watermelon belly. A good number of community folk felt the need to get out of bed and get the news about Jake's wife first hand when he phoned home from the hospital, telling his mother-in-law that it was a boy and a girl.

Some folks got quite upset when they were on the phone and they knew that their neighbours were *schnacking opp*. Too many eavesdroppers on the line at one time reduced the quality of the sound. There were clues that told who was *schnacking opp*. When Helena was *schnacking opp*, her husband's cuckoo clock announced every half-hour in the background. The cuckoo may as well have said "*de Jon Sawatsche schnackt opp* (Mrs. Johan Sawatzky is eavesdropping)." Another neighbour was identified by her heavy asthmatic breathing and yet another was identified by her children calling "*Mama, ons kjleena Willie es aulwada naut* (Mama, our little Willie is wet again)."

When the sound quality got so poor that it was near impossible to hear the voice at the other end of the line, the caller would say, "*Ejk wud die bäta heare kjenne wan eensje Lied wudde opp henje* (I would be able to hear you better if some people would hang up)." Immediately "click, click, click" was heard as the receivers on the party line were hung up in households along the line.

One thing for sure, knowing what was going on in the district was very important. Privacy and confidentiality were not nearly as important as being on top of the local news.

Endnotes

Where They Came From

Katharina and Peter S. Hildebrand and Helena and Johan M. Sawatzky were all children of Mennonite immigrants who had left the rich southern Russian breadbasket (Ukraine) in 1874 and 1875 to start a new life in Canada.

Genogram of the Hildebrand family:

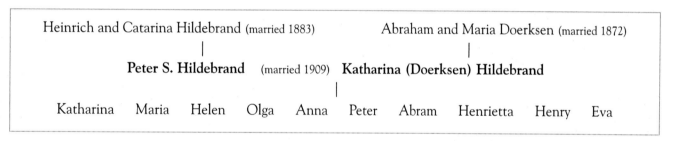

Heinrich and Catarina Hildebrand (married 1883)   Abraham and Maria Doerksen (married 1872)

Peter S. Hildebrand   (married 1909)   **Katharina (Doerksen) Hildebrand**

Katharina   Maria   Helen   Olga   Anna   Peter   Abram   Henrietta   Henry   Eva

Genogram of the Sawatzky family:

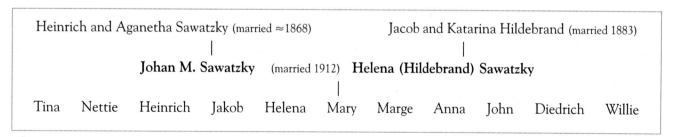

Heinrich and Aganetha Sawatzky (married ≈1868)   Jacob and Katarina Hildebrand (married 1883)

Johan M. Sawatzky   (married 1912)   **Helena (Hildebrand) Sawatzky**

Tina   Nettie   Heinrich   Jakob   Helena   Mary   Marge   Anna   John   Diedrich   Willie

Katharina Doerksen and Peter S. Hildebrand were married November 11, 1909 in the village of Sommerfeld, where they had both grown up. They moved to the nearby school district of Edenburg where Peter's father had purchased land earlier that spring. Peter and Katharina raised their ten children in Edenburg. They were: Katharina 1910, Maria 1912, Helena (Helen) 1914, Olga 1915, Anna 1918, Peter 1920, Abram (who later changed his name to Alan) 1922, Henrietta 1925, Heinrich (Henry) 1927, and Eva 1930.

Peter S. Hildebrand's parents were Heinrich Hildebrand and Catarina Sawatzke (both were born in 1862). Heinrich was 12 years old when he came to Canada with his parents and nine siblings in July, 1874. The Hildebrand family came to Canada from Russia, via Fargo, North Dakota. They were travelling from Fargo to Manitoba on the Red River in the riverboat The International when Heinrich, who was holding his sickly little brother Abraham, fell into the river, brother and all. Fortunately, a worker on a passing barge

Peter S. and Katharina Hildebrand

witnessed the fall and pulled the two lads out of the water. Heinrich was unconscious, but still had a tight grip on his little brother.

Catarina Sawatzke arrived in Canada in 1875. Initially her family also settled in the Fargo area. Catarina's mother had died when Catarina was one year old. Her father had remarried, and Catarina's new stepmother often spanked her with an angle iron on her bare backside. After Catarina's father died, her uncle Peter Sawatzky took the fifteen-year-old Catarina to Canada with him and the rest of his family. For one week, they walked from Fargo to Manitoba, chasing a herd of cattle that they brought with them. It was late fall, and Catarina remembered how the bottoms of the women's long skirts were often frozen stiff as boards from the cold wet weather. Catarina was hired by a family who not only employed her, but also treated her as their own daughter. Her salary of $35.00 the first year, and $45.00 the second year, was small compared to the "family" that they gave her.

Heinrich and Catarina were married on December 11, 1883. They raised their family in the newly established village of Sommerfeld, Manitoba.

Katharina Hildebrand's parents were Abraham and Maria (born 1852 and 1855 respectively) Doerksen. Two years after they were married, they came to Canada with a one-year-old daughter in 1874. When they first arrived in Canada, they settled in the Mennonite East Reserve. In 1880, they applied to homestead in Sommerfeld. They moved to Sommerfeld, where they raised their family of ten surviving children. Abraham and Maria Doerksen originally came from the Bergthal Colony near Mariopul, a port city on the Sea of Azov in Russia (Ukraine). Abraham was ordained as bishop of the Sommerfeld Mennonite Church in 1894.

Johan M. and Helena Sawatzky

Helena Hildebrand and Johan M. Sawatzky were also married in Sommerfeld. Johan was raised in the nearby district of Halbstadt, and Helena was raised in the village of Sommerfeld. Helena's next door neighbour, Bishop Abraham Doerksen, the father of Katharina Doerksen Hildebrand, married them on November 7, 1912. Bishop Doerksen's sermon at their wedding was taken from the Book of Ruth, Chapter 1 Verse 16. It read, "But Ruth said, entreat me not to leave you or return from following you for where you go, I will go, and where you lodge I will lodge; your people shall be my people and your God my God."

Helena and Johan M. moved to the district of Blumenthal, about four miles east of Sommerfeld. They had fourteen children. They were: Katharina (Tina) 1913, Aganetha (Nettie) 1916, Heinrich 1918, Jakob 1920, Helena 1922, Maria (Mary) 1924, Margaretha (Marge) 1926, Anna 1927, Johann (John) 1929, Diedrich 1932, and Wilhelm (Willie) 1935. Cornelius and Peter (1932) were twins. Cornelius lived 3 1/2 hours and Peter lived

40 minutes. David (1939) was stillborn.

Johan M. Sawatzky's father, Heinrich Sawatzky and mother, Aganetha nee Martens (born 1848 and 1849 respectively) married around 1868. They arrived in Canada in 1875 and settled in the district of Halbstadt, about three miles southeast of Sommerfeld.

Helena Sawatzky's mother was Katarina Sawatzky (born 1869). Her father, Jacob Hildebrand (born 1860) came to Canada in 1874 at the age of 14. He arrived with his parents, Peter Hildebrand and Katharina Neufeldt (born 1831 and 1832 respectively), and his siblings including his brother Heinrich Hildebrand, who later became the father of Peter S. Hildebrand.

There were a number of reasons why many Mennonites, including the parents of Peter S. and Katharina Hildebrand and Johan M. and Helena Sawatzky left Russia (Ukraine) in the late 1800s. Young men who wanted to start farming in Russia could not buy land because there was not enough available land. There was a new law in Russia that no longer exempted Mennonite men from military service. Mennonites were pacifists and could not take up arms to participate in military service.

They searched for a place where they would not be required to serve in the army and where they could own farmland. In 1872 the Canadian government sent Mr. William Hespeler to Russia. He personally invited the Mennonites to settle in Canada. Canada needed settlers for the western prairies.

A delegation of twelve Mennonite men visited Canada in 1873. They determined that Canada was a good place for the Mennonites to settle. The Canadian government promised a quarter section (160 acres) of free land to each settler over 21 years of age. If they settled on the land, they were allowed to buy the other three-quarter section for one dollar an acre.

In addition, Canada assured the Mennonites that their young men would be exempt from military service; that they could operate their schools in the German language without government interference; and that they were free to practice their own religion.

Of the approximately 18,000 people who left Ukraine in the 1870s, about 7,000 came to Manitoba. Many more Mennonites followed them in subsequent years. This is well documented in numerous books and scholarly papers.

Thank You

I sent my nephew Micheal a copy of stories that I had written for a Sawatzky family gathering in July 2001. After he had read the stories, he called his sister Michele and asked, "Is this for real?" This lightning rod guided me to write more family stories.

Collecting the stories from my parents, aunts, uncles and cousins evolved into an incredible journey. I heard stories that I do not remember. Listening to stories over many a *Faspa* has truly been a gift to me. I do hope that everyone enjoyed telling the stories as much as I enjoyed hearing them.

My sincere thanks go to the many people who have shared their stories with me. They are: my parents, Henry and Anna Hildebrand; my aunts and uncles, Nettie Neufeld, Jakob, John, Dick and Bill Sawatzky, Mary Hildebrand, Helen Friesen, Olga Sawatzky, Peter and Doris Hildebrand, Henrietta Schroeder, Eva Hiebert; and those who have passed on and left their stories behind, Anne Schellenberg, Helen Krueger, Alan Hildebrand, Maria Wiebe, Heinrich Sawatzky, Tina Friesen, Marge Hildebrand and my grandparents. Thank you to George Wall and Dave Hildebrand who took time to tell me about sparrows and garden paths over cups of coffee; to Peter Hildebrand for sharing his experience of blackmail; and to Dora Penner for shedding light on bloodletting.

My appreciation goes to the many generous family and friends who have read the stories and offered suggestions. Niomie Penner provided helpful ideas and thoughts when I got stuck. Pamela Hunter offered suggestions and said nice things about the stories. Henry Dyck encouraged me and reminded me to put the stories into context. Anna Rojas Flores worked tirelessly on edits and helped sort out those pesky commas. Edith Friesen gave many helpful editorial suggestions. Ted Klassen encouraged me to tell the stories. Joanne Klassen planted the seed and said I could do it. Katie Altendorf Cable let her creativity flow into the beautiful illustrations. Jan Funk and Dawn Wilson of Interior Publishing & Communication Ltd. put the polish on *Faspa*. Myra and Larry Danielson, Betty Ann Zegarac, and Betty Lou Anderson offered sage advice as they scanned the pages between the covers.

My heartfelt gratitude goes to my sisters Elaine, Debbie, Brenda and my brother, Henry Dale and my other brother, Henry Lavern. They presented me with nieces and nephews and the reason to write these stories.

To Larry, my life partner, for walking beside me every step of this journey; for his tears and his belly laughs when I read him the stories; for never doubting that *Faspa* would come to be; and for escaping to the golf course when I needed quiet working time. Thank you from my heart.

Honourable Mentions

The source of *Plautdietsch* (Low German) spelling and definitions was:
Rempel, H. (1984). <u>*Kjenn Jie Noch Plautdietch – A Mennonite Low German Dictionary*</u>. Altona, Manitoba, Canada: Friesen Printers.

Enns, F. G. (1987). <u>Gretna, Window on the Northwest</u>. Altona, Manitoba, Canada: D. W. Friesen & Sons Ltd.

Permission was granted to print line drawings from <u>Good Old Days Colouring Book</u> by Valley Harvest Maids. Copyright ©1997 by Pembina Threshermans Museum.

The following stories were previously published by the author:

Chornoboy, E. (2000). Balloons and Henrietta's Stooks. Cuthbert Y. and McCallister, J. sponsored by Manitoba Farm Women's Conference, <u>Around the Kitchen Table</u>. Altona, Manitoba, Canada: Friesen's Book Division.

Chornoboy, E. (2002). The Telegram. <u>Heartspace Writing school. Beyond Words: Heartspace Writing School Anthology 2002.</u> Winnipeg, Manitoba, Canada: Interior Publishing & Communication Ltd.

Chornoboy, E. (2003). My Boys are Doing Good and *Tweede Heljedach* entitled "Boxing Day". <u>Seasons of the Heart, Heartspace Anthology 2003.</u> Winnipeg, Canada: Interior Publishing & Communication Ltd.

Eleanor Hildebrand Chornoboy is a native of southern Manitoba. She grew up on the family farm in the school district of Edenburg where she attended school in the one-room schoolhouse. She received her high school education at the Mennonite Collegiate Institute in Gretna, Manitoba, and received her teaching credentials, a Bachelor's Degree and a Master's Degree in Family Studies at the University of Manitoba. Her professional life has been dedicated to children with special needs and their families, working towards the inclusion of all children who are gifted with different strengths.

Over the years, Eleanor has collected and documented family stories. Initially she collected the stories for her own curiosity and interest, but soon she realized that many of the stories were unknown to her generation, and to the young people in her life. She believes that if the stories and anecdotes are not documented, they will be lost. To tell the stories is her opportunity to let the children know about those who came before them.